Anthony Gregory

Life on the Leicester Line

The Progress of a Train Driver

Acknowledgements

I would like to thank the following people for their contributions to this book. David Wright for his lovely map of the branch; Ian Farnfield for careful reading of the proofs; John Tuffs, Karl Brailsford, Robert Woodman, Tony Overton, John Oldershaw and the late Bert Wynn for supplying photographs.

My appreciation has to go to all those fine railwaymen and characters who worked on the branch, without whom this book would not have been possible. In particular, former Coalville depot manager David Kirk; Colin Hadley (former branch secretary); and Dennis Wright (Guards LDC) for their written contributions.

Special thanks also to Nicholas Whittaker for his painstaking editorial work and advice on the publication of this book.

Last but not least my family, my wife Lorraine and children James, Abbie and Thomas for their patience and assistance during the book's writing and production.

Anthony Gregory, Burton-on-Trent, 2002

James Gregory for proof reading the updated version of this book and Brian Whiteford for getting it into printable format.

Anthony Gregory, Burton-on-Trent, 2017

Front Cover photographs:

56037 with (left to right) Ray Cooper, Harold Booth, Pat Maund, Ray Leer, Stan Webb and Tommy Hall. *Photo: Steve Marks*

20007 with (left to right) Frank Wood and Frank Bailey. *Photo: John Oldershaw.*

Last night at Mantle Lane Box with (left to right) Rob Kelsall, Tony Parker, Phil Gamble, Carl Southwood, Tony Overton, Nigel Wilkins, Anthony Gregory and Mick Badder. *Photo: Nigel Walker for author.*

Back cover photograph:

Author Anthony Gregory on board 47401 (ex D 1500) after bringing locos for the 1990 Coalville Open Day. *Photo: Dennis Wright.*

(DEDICATION)

In Memory of Betty and Harry Gregory
My Parents

Contents

Introduction

I have been asked by Tony Gregory to write a few lines on the closure of Coalville MPD. For two years prior to closure the morale of the drivers had been declining along with the available work. Weekly coal traffic slowly declined from a peak of about 145,000 tonnes to 45,000 tonnes. Coalville was one of the few depots on British Rail that actually made a profit - about £1 million a week at its peak.

At one union-management meeting we'd been told that Coalville depot's future was assured. But it is my belief that a decision on the future of coal was forced on management by ASLEF sectional council concerned with low morale. It also has to be said that the politics of coal was a major factor in the decision to close. As usual a précis was produced in May 1990 highlighting the potential savings that could be made from more flexibility and utilisation of resources. I do not believe that any other depot could offer the service, flexibility or utilisation of resources that Coalville men could. Our only disadvantage was having to rely on the ferrying of locomotives for fuel servicing and repairs.

I feel bound to thank our Freight Services Manager, Mr Ian Mansfield, for giving us every opportunity and assistance in putting together a case for saving Coalville from closure. It was never going to be a fight to the finish. All we wanted was a reasonable compromise whereby substantial savings were offered in return for the promise of a safe future free from the ongoing threat of closure, with expectation of reasonable job satisfaction for staff who remained. The, savings demanded by management - £478,113 per annum - were parried by our very reasonable offer of £403,383, to which we added the following rationale:

It is a great pity that the decision to close Coalville has come at this time, especially in the light of proposals now before various bodies regarding permission to extract coal which would have significant bearing on the viability of keeping Coalville as a train crew depot.

Although our final figures showing potential savings that could be made at Coalville show a shortfall against the management figure, there are costs for which management have not allowed. We have pointed out these costs but been unable to furnish exact figures. But when taken into account we believe that our proposals far outweigh the savings, flexibility and customer service demanded by management.

At the end of the day management were not prepared to offer any guarantees for our future and sadly we had to accept closure. Seven drivers retired, seventeen drivers went to Toton, four to Nottingham, six to Leicester, one to Birmingham New Street, two to Saltley, two to Bescot, one to Derby. Two resigned. Three of the trainmen 'D' went to Toton and two to Leicester.

My twelve years ten months spent at Coalville were the best of my railway career to date and I would like to take this opportunity to thank everyone I worked with over the years for their help, advice and friendship.

Colin Hadley, ASLEF branch secretary/LDC 'B' of Coalville branch
1988 - until closure on 1st October 1990.

PREFACE

I first became involved with the Coalville depot when I was appointed as Traffic Assistant (later changed to Traffic Manager) in 1974. I had already been with British Railways for 20 years and had previously been a station master, Yard Supervisor at Chaddesden Marshalling Yard and Operating Supervisor at Wirksworth before arriving at Coalville.

In 1974 (and indeed for the next ten years) the depot was responsible for the movement of around 100,000 tonnes of coal per week from Leicestershire and South Derbyshire collieries to power stations along the Trent Valley and also to Didcot. There was also (and still is) a large traffic flow of stone from the quarries at Cliffe Hill and Bardon Hill to various destinations in block trains. A twice-weekly train of bitumen tanks from Ellesmere Port to Bardon Hill for Prismo also ran. All of this traffic was the very reason for the depot at Coalville.

The section of line between Knighton South junction and Burton on Trent with its six signalboxes, Coalville depot, the truncated branches to Measham and Cadley Hill colliery and the power station at Drakelow became my responsibility.

The depot was unusual in that the train crew, shunters and yard staff all shared the mess room and other facilities. This seemed to work well and the mix of the staff gave a better understanding of each other's duties and problems. They all knew that their jobs and the depot itself were sustained by the high tonnage from the collieries and that their future lay in keeping it on the move. But Coalville - as on British Railways generally - always faced a shortage of resources, locomotives and men. At times it was a great struggle to meet all of the customer's requirements and a great deal of ingenuity was shown by supervisors and men to keep the job running in all weathers and despite all difficulties.

I was always pleased to meet with the staff's elected representatives the Local Departmental Committee (LDC) which had separate committees for drivers and for guards. I have always believed that good staff relations are essential to the running of any depot. We did not always agree but always had mutual respect for each other's point of view. This came to the fore during the dark days of the Miners strike in 1983/84. I had firm instructions to move as much coal as possible and the staff were instructed by their Trade Unions not to do so. Despite the pressures relations between the staff and myself remained good and did not change. This says a lot for the staff and the depot.

An important event in the life of the depot was the annual Open Day, which I have covered, in a separate chapter in the book. I feel particularly proud to have been part of this, which in my view was a boost for the depot and the staff and really put it on the map. Though I left Coalville

Depot in 1984 I continued to chair the Open Day Committee until the final one was held in 1991. By this time the collieries had closed and the subsequent loss of traffic meant that the depot could no longer be sustained. The depot had officially closed before the 1991 Open Day but this was specially agreed to be the last.

So ended an era. Coalville depot was a special and rather unique depot, still greatly missed by the staff who worked there and the thousands who came and enjoyed the Open Days.

Anthony Gregory has done a fine job in bringing together the stories of the depot of Coalville and I wish him every success.

David J Kirk BEM, April 2002.

1: The Hand of Fate

My first hands-on experience of loco driving came one summer evening in 1974. Four of us had cycled down to Moor Street, as we did most nights, and ventured along the path that led to the MPD or 'the loco' as it was known. Just before the MPD entrance there was a dirty old stream with a makeshift bridge made of old railway sleepers. As we crossed it we could see the train crew cabin with its collection of drivers, guards and second men. Leaning our bikes against the wall, we walked along to the foreman's office to ask if we could go round the depot. It was always a tense moment, as you never knew what the answer would be. A gruff 'No, clear off!' was the usual response - but this time we were lucky.

'Alright, wait there, I'll get somebody to show you round.'

Normally we'd end up with some miserable old chap who was just about to go home and eager for a pint or his bed. But the young driver who came out to us was full of enthusiasm.

'Come on then lads, let's take you round.'

We followed him round, scribbling down the numbers of the various locos on our pads. Once we had finished he took us over to a line of Brush 4s - or Class 47s as we know them today.

'Get up in the cab and I'll show you round,' he said.

Ding! He flicked a switch and we climbed aboard. We watched fascinated as he put in his key. A high-pitched whine came from the engine room. When that stopped he pressed a button and the big diesel engine roared into life. All the time he was explaining the various switches, dials and levers and which one did what. Eventually he unpegged the brake.

One of you get in the seat then,' he said.

The four of us looked at each other with worried faces. Someone pushed me from behind and I couldn't help but take a step forward to 'volunteer.'

'Come on, don't be shy.'

I jumped into the seat and as my mates stood there grinning he gave me step-by-step instructions on how to drive the loco.

'Right, that there's the power handle. Pull it back towards you.'

I did as instructed.

'Not too much!' he yelled. 'Else we'll jump over the loco in front!'

I eased the handle back, more steadily this time and suddenly we were trundling along the road. I couldn't believe it - I was actually driving a railway engine!

'That's it,' he said encouragingly. 'We'll make a driver of you yet.'

After giving me instructions on how to brake he brought the lesson to a close.

Class 20s on Burton loco 1978. Photo: John Tuffs.

'Thank you,' I said timidly.

He took over from me and drove the Brush 4 back to its original position and shut down the engine.

As we walked back to the shed buildings I told him about my uncle, Charlie Buckley, who was also a Burton driver.

'Charlie? Oh yes, we know Charlie. He's a bit of a character down here.'

If only I'd had a penny for every time I was to hear that statement in the years to come! After thanking the young man again, we collected our bikes and started back for Moor Street Bridge where the rest of the trainspotting crowd gathered. At the time I could have punched whoever had pushed me forward - but today I remain forever grateful for the memory. I call it the hand of fate!

As the years went on we got to know a lot of the men at Burton sheds. Sometimes we would help them by pulling the point handles for them - and in return we would get a cab ride down to the berthing point.

Burton sheds closed as a booking-on point in 1975. Many men - including my Uncle Charlie - retired from the railways for good, while others went to Derby or Coalville. Burton remained open as a fuelling point until late 1981, manned by just a shed driver and second man. But that's a story that I'll continue later...

2: A Lucky Break

My first job after I left school in 1977, was at a dairy farm in Rolleston-on-Dove. I'd always loved the countryside, so I figured that it would be ideal...

The six-mile bike ride wouldn't have been a hardship in good weather, but on my first day it teemed with rain. The second day brought a hard frost. And on my third and final day the countryside was blanketed in snow. Farmer Thompson had a habit of leaving me alone all day - but not without first handing me a long list of heavy tasks. At lunchtime on Wednesday I sat on a bale of hay thinking about my old schoolmates and feeling nostalgic for our trainspotting days. As I bit into my cold egg sandwich - watched by four big dirty black rats! - I heard a train go by in the distance.

'That's it,' I thought. 'This isn't for me.'

I decided to leave there and then - but not before I nearly got crushed by a huge Friesian cow! Farmer Thompson paid me fifteen pounds for my three days of farm life and I headed off back to the Job Centre.

My next job brought me a step nearer to the railway, helping to move a cash 'n' carry firm to new premises across the line from Burton MPD. Ten of us were set on, with the promise of a permanent job for the hardest-working pair. For the first time in my life I got lucky and was one of the chosen two.

One day sticks in my mind. At lunchtime I used to take my sandwiches round to Moor Street Bridge and watch the trains. At ten to two, one of the canteen ladies would come along and I would walk with her back to the cash 'n' carry, pushing my bike. On this particular day we'd just started heading back when a man rushed past us from the opposite direction. Never had I seen such a look on anyone's face - it can only be described as insanity. He stumbled by and scaled the dirt bank leading up to the railway line.

'He's a rum looking perisher,' the canteen lady exclaimed.

I couldn't help but agree, but as we neared the cash n carry we put it out of our minds.

My first job of the afternoon was to accompany the assistant manager to the bank with the morning's takings. As we passed the railway station we noticed a police car and an ambulance, but didn't think that much of it until we got back to work and saw people milling around the fence that separated the cash 'n' carry from the railway. I went over to see what was happening. Two policemen stood watching as a group of ambulancemen picked up something from off the tracks.

'It's a body,' someone said.

The canteen lady came up behind me and tapped me on the arm.

'It's that bloke we saw at dinnertime.'

I could only stand and stare, thinking that the man had been alive just an hour before. The loco that had ended his life was a Mini Brush - or Class 31. It had to be detached from its train and taken on to Burton sheds to be cleaned.

As the months went by I continued to spend my lunchtimes at Moor Street Bridge. Autumn had arrived and it was getting colder. One day - in October 1978 - I stood watching as a set of engines came off the Leicester line and stopped at Moor Street. They were preparing to go back into Burton sheds and the crew had to change ends. As they walked by me they gave a cheery greeting, which I returned. Watching the loco trundle off I couldn't help but envy the driver's mate.

'Lucky devil,' I thought. 'And he's only about my age. I'd love a job like that.'

Suddenly I had the idea that a job on the railways was what I wanted. Any job would do me. With that thought I jumped on my bike and headed for the coal wharf offices where the local permanent way gang was based. Leaning my bike against the wall I knocked on the door of an open passageway. From somewhere inside a voice called out.

'Come in, I'm down here.'

I walked along the passageway and came to the only occupied office.

'In here, mate.'

I walked in. The office smelled old and fusty and was piled high with unfinished paperwork, books, maps and other railway artefacts.

'Blast this paperwork,' the man grumbled. 'It's coming out of my ears.'

'I've just come to see if there's any vacancies as a platelayer,' I explained.

He looked up and took off his glasses.

'Well, that's a coincidence. We're advertising vacancies next Monday.'

Standing up he opened a grey filing cabinet and took out some application forms. I began to feel excited. I'd really struck lucky!

'Fill these in,' he said. 'Name, address, phone number if you've got one. Do you mind shift work?'

I shook my head and carried on writing down my details.

'By the way,' he asked. 'How old are you?'

'Sixteen.'

With that he took off his glasses and screwed up my freshly completed form. He looked irritated.

'Sorry, son, but you have to be eighteen to work on the line.'

I must have looked devastated, because he seemed to soften and take pity on me.

'Look, if it's a job on the railways you want, I've got an address here. You can apply to become a traction trainee.'

'What's one of them?' I asked.

'I think it's the first step on the way to being a train driver.'

I took the address and thanked him for his trouble. Back at the cash 'n' carry I spent all afternoon unable to stop thinking about the day's events. How great it would be to achieve one of my greatest ambitions...

Later that evening I wrote a letter to the address he'd given me, explaining my lifelong interest in the railways and how much I'd love a job with them. I posted it on my way to work the next morning but couldn't help thinking it would probably come to nothing.

Two weeks later a letter arrived from the Area Manager. Second men - drivers' assistants - were required for the depots at Derby and Coalville and he would contact me shortly to arrange an interview date. I could hardly believe my luck. But even then I didn't dare take things for granted. So many of my ambitions had a nasty habit of falling at the first hurdle.

3: The Job Interview

In the second week of November British Rail sent me a letter asking me to attend a formal interview and induction test. Attached was a free ticket to Derby where the interviews were being held.

I put in for a day off from the cash 'n' carry (without telling them what it was for!) and when the big day came I dressed as smartly as I could and set off. My destination - Wyvern House - was a large pile of offices at the end of Derby station's Platform One. A secretary told me to take a seat in the waiting room with two other lads. We chatted for a while, as the secretary came to fetch each of us in turn.

When my turn came I was shown into a large office decked out with paintings of steam locos and hedged in by shelves full of thick books. The room smelled of a bygone age, as if it had remained unchanged since the turn of the century. Two large well-dressed men in trilby hats looked me over from the other side of a highly polished desk.

'This one's Gregory,' one of them grunted to the other.

'Come in Gregory. Take a seat.'

Nervously I sat down.

'Now then Gregory, why do you want to join British Rail?'

I told him that I'd had a keen interest in railways for eight years and it had always been my ambition to be a driver. They nodded at each other, seemingly satisfied with my answer. Next came the question, how would I get to the depot if I was given a job?

'I'd buy a motorbike?'

'Hmm.' They looked a bit dubious. 'And what if it went wrong?'

'I'd learn how to repair it.'

Again they nodded approval. Ten minutes later and I was still struggling through their questions. After what seemed like an age the man who had questioned me so thoroughly turned to his colleague and asked him if he had anything to ask me. The second man suddenly sat upright and glared at me.

'Right, let's just say you got this job. You're with a driver on shed, preparing locos for other drivers. Your driver comes and asks you to sweep out the cab. Would you tell him to piss off or would you do it?'

His language shocked me, but I swallowed hard and thought quickly.

'Yes, I'd do it, as the driver would be like the boss of you anyway.'

'Right, no more questions, ' he said.

Sensing that I'd said the right thing I began to relax.

'Right, Mr Gregory, send in the last one and wait until he comes out. Then the three of you can sit the test.'

Test? I didn't like the sound of that at all. But he'd called me Mister for the first time and I guessed that was a good sign.

Some of the test questions I flew through, but others I stumbled over. Still, I managed to have a go at all of them. When the papers were taken away, the three of us lads sat talking quietly amongst ourselves. Eventually the more official-looking of the two large gentlemen came back into the room.

'Thank you all for coming along today,' he said. 'You will hear from us shortly regarding the outcome of your interviews.'

Feeling a bit disappointed we left. We'd all hoped to know our results straight away. But it didn't work that way on the railways!

A week or so later a brown envelope dropped through my letterbox. As I ripped it open I could see straight away where it was from. But what would it say?

'We are pleased to inform you...' A good start! I guessed the rest, but read on anyway. 'A medical has been arranged for you on the above date.'

A medical! Something else to worry about. But the day arrived quickly enough and armed with another free ticket , I set off to Derby to see the railway doctor. It meant another day's leave, so I was hoping it would all be worth it.

The medical was stringent, with eyesight, hearing and blood pressure tests amongst others. After leaving a urine sample the doctor told me I'd have my results through in a few days. More disappointment. More waiting. But, sure enough, a few days later another letter informed me that I'd passed all the necessary requirements and could now be offered a job at Coalville depot. To say I was thrilled was an understatement! At last I had achieved something worthwhile.

First of all I had to attend a formal chat at Wyvern House to discuss the procedures and pick up various railway booklets, a high-visibility vest and a free pass to Leicester where a six-week traction trainee course was due to start on the 15th January 1979.

The only thing left for me to do was hand in my notice at the cash 'n' carry. I finished on Christmas Eve and spent my last afternoon at the Coopers Arms in the company of all the friends I'd made. I was sad to be leaving, but I knew I was moving on to better things. Now all I needed to do was to cycle over to Coalville to check out my new workplace. And to enjoy my Christmas of course.

4: My First Trip To Coalville

The Christmas break of 1978 arrived and, as usual, I enjoyed myself to the full. Just one thing weighed on my mind: in a few weeks time I would be starting a new job in a strange town with people I'd never met. To banish the butterflies I tried to tell myself that I'd be alright and I'd rise to the occasion, just as I always did.

Christmas Day came and went and ushered in that dreary interval between the end of festivities and the new year. I decided to make my visit to Coalville on New Year's Eve, figuring that the roads would be quiet. That Sunday morning was frosty but sunny, and by early afternoon the streets were aired and the chill had gone. I looked forward to a pleasant ride.

To pass the long 17-mile ride I began to think back to my early associations with the railways…

Like one time in the mid-Sixties, on a train going on our holidays, when Dad lifted me up to the carriage window so I could look out. The entire length of the train seemed to stretch out in front of us as we banked into a tight curve. From the steam loco at the front grey smoke and white steam billowed into the blue sky and left little clouds hanging over the green fields.

And I thought about the days, aged about ten, when my mates and I spent hours on the iron bridge at Stapenhill watching the heavy coal trains going into Drakelow Power Station. The trains seemed to be constant - coal and stone in one direction, echoing empties in another - all passing below us and filling our young nostrils with heady blue diesel fumes.

Drakelow and the surrounding area were where we all grew up as tatty kids and where, in 1972, I had my very first cab ride. The crew were Coalville men and the loco was 47315. From then on, in all my trainspotting books, that number was proudly accompanied by the letters C.R. for cab ride. A short one maybe - just from the sidings to the east departure signal - but for an 11-year-old it was an unforgettable thrill.

Another haunt of ours was Cadley Hill Colliery, where small saddle tank steam locos still operated. We would spend hours watching them shunt their NCB and mainline trucks. The crews soon got to know us and one day we were invited up onto the footplate of one of the locos. We chatted pleasantly to both driver and fireman as they explained to us what each control did.

'Well, we can't stop nattering all day, lads – we've got work to do.'

Disappointed by our all-too-brief visit we prepared to dismount from the footplate. The driver burst into laughter.

'Nah, lads, you can stop on if you like. Just stand still and keep out of the way and you'll be fine.'

And so we spent the whole afternoon on that engine. They even let us fire it for a while. It would have been nice to have a go at driving. Alas they didn't let us go that far, but it remains an unforgettable memory.

Then came my trainspotting days proper. All the years spent at Moor Street Bridge, on the path used by the train crews between the railway sheds and Burton station. From 1971 this was our regular stomping ground and we must have spent hundreds of happy hours there. We also made day trips out, starting small at Derby and Tamworth, then gradually moving further to destinations like Birmingham and Sheffield. Before too long we were venturing as far afield as London or Scotland. We kept the truth of our jaunts from our parents: if they'd known our plans they'd soon have put a stop to our gallivanting! But we knew there was safety in numbers – between six and eight of us usually – and we stuck together like glue.

My last cab ride before starting work on the railways was in 1976, on the footplate of a Class 45 'Peak' between Birmingham New Street and Saltley depot.

But those things were all in my past. 'This is my future,' I thought as I passed a large road sign announcing Coalville…

The sun was beginning to set in a watery sky as I arrived at the depot. Not that it looked much like a depot to me – not like the ones at Derby or Toton with their huge maintenance sheds and fuelling points. Still, it had a local signal box and a train crew building and rows of silent engines. I walked around the deserted depot, peeped into the mess room and generally explored the place. As I sat on a buffer stop to take a rest I thought 'yes, I think I could be happy here.' Around me in neat rows were white paraffin tail-lights. Leant against the buffer stops were shunting poles and break sticks.

The day was beginning to get chilly as I walked back to my bike. Bending down I picked up a copy of the ASLEF Rule Book from the ground and slipped it into my pocket. Looking back one more time I left to begin my lonely ride home. But it had put my mind at rest to see my new place of work. Would it be here where all my ambitions would be realised? It remained to be seen…

In 1984, 58009 leaves by the east departure below the iron bridge - where it all began. Photo John Tuffs.

5: Traction Training

The first weeks of 1979 brought severe frost and snow. On the 15th January, in order to get to Leicester on time, I had to get the 05.05 mail train from Burton to Derby - a service known by railwaymen as 'The Rabbits'. Once at Derby I found myself a seat in a warm DMU - but its departure was heavily delayed because of the weather. So on my very first morning, despite my early start, I arrived late.

Walking down the path at Beal Street I could feel the nerves tensing in my stomach. I braced myself and knocked on the door of the small classroom that had been put aside for us.

'Come in!'

I pushed the door open and was immediately aware of fifteen pairs of eyes looking at me.

'Is it Tony?' asked the man at the front of the class. 'Tony Gregory?'

I nodded and mumbled something about a late train.

'Not to worry, Tony. Sit down over there. That's your place.'

He continued with his short introduction. After a while I began to feel better and took time to look around at my classmates. I could see the tall lad I'd been at the interview with, but not the other one. I guessed he'd failed and it struck me as somewhat ironic as he was the only one of us who actually lived in Coalville!

Our instructor turned out to be the popular Bernard Willis. In the years to come he would take us for several other courses and was the most competent instructor I've ever been taught by. His back-ups were Bill Soden and Dennis Simpson, the latter being one of the proper locomen of our era in my estimation..
Our first day turned out to be relaxed and light-hearted. Alongside us trainees for Coalville, were others destined for Leicester and Nottingham. As most of them were good lads it wasn't long before we were all chatting freely. We were also treated to an early hometime. Thus concluded a very reassuring start to our new careers.

The next day was not so good. ASLEF, the train driver's union, were holding a series of one-day strikes on the Tuesday and Thursday of each week. It messed up our travel plans, but we had no bad feelings about it. These were the chaps whose ranks we'd be joining eventually. But my own journeys became a nightmare! I still had to be up at 4 a.m., but instead of a short cycle ride to Burton station I now faced a three-mile trek to Wetmore Bus Park. Once on the bus there was an expensive fare and a long boring journey through countless small villages. By the time we reached Markfield the bus was filling up with workers on their way to Leicester. Alighting at the station I made my way to Beal Street. We now had to get some work done, so by the time I'd finished it was teatime.

The tall lad - who I now knew as Craig - lived locally and gave me directions back to the bus station. The bus was packed, but I was just glad to be heading home again. After half an hour the passengers thinned out so I relaxed in a nice warm seat and soon afterwards dropped into a welcome sleep. A rude awakening was inevitable at Wetmore Bus Park and I had to face a three mile walk back home again. By the time I sat down to a welcome tea it was well past six o'clock!

Thursday was even worse and my morning trek was made all the more miserable by snow and a freezing wind. My shoes leaked and my feet quickly turned to ice! At the bus park I bought a newspaper to stave off the boredom - but it was still dark and so blustery that reading was impossible. I didn't start to read it until we were approaching the stop where the bus normally filled up. As we wound our way round the endless lanes again I began to feel dizzy. The more I tried to concentrate on my paper, the worse it got. The murmur of voices and the smells of cigarette smoke and perfume made me feel so sick that I wanted to get off. But we were only on the outskirts of Leicester: if I got off now I'd be lost in no time. I don't know how I managed to hang on, but I did. Even to this day I cannot read while I'm in a road vehicle - though I have no problems on a train!

After another long day with more travel problems I eventually got back to Burton at 8 p.m. Luckily for me - and thousands of other passengers - the ASLEF strike was resolved that same week.

The next week would be different again. Bernard had sussed out who were the true enthusiasts and who weren't. We would leave the classroom about 3 p.m. to catch the express to Derby. Three parts of our class used this train, including Bernard. While the Nottingham lads would scuttle off to the buffet, the rest would hang about in the corridor chatting. One afternoon, as we waited for the train, Bernard asked if anyone would like to gain some experience by riding in the loco cab. Surprisingly no one seemed that bothered, so I said I'd be happy to give it a go - especially as the train was usually headed by a Class 45 'Peak' loco. They were my favourite, a proper diesel locomotive of my generation. I'd classed them twice already - but a cab ride, now that really would be something else! Once the train came to a halt Bernard went over to the loco and opened the cab door.

'Hello Ray, I've got a traction trainee here going to Derby. Can he ride with you?'

'Sure, Bernard.'

'See you tomorrow, Tony,' said Bernard, and with that he pushed me inside and slammed the solid heavy door shut.

'Sit down, lad,' said the driver. 'There's no second man booked on this job.'

Suddenly I heard the shrill note of a whistle and caught the flash of a green flag. We were off. As the driver slammed the power handle onto 'Full' the Peak surged forward with a loud roar. We were soon up to 90 mph. It was my first look into the day-to-day realities of working on the railways. Everything was in place: a powerful diesel running under semaphore signals, with one of the 'old school' at the controls. It turned out that our driver was an ex-Burton man, many of whom had gone to Derby in 1975 when 16F closed.

As the weeks went on we undertook several courses, including a first aid course where we practised the kiss of life on 'Little Annie' - a rubber dummy which consisted of only head and shoulders! - and a fire prevention exercise involving the usual burning tin and fire extinguishers.

Most of our time though was spent with a pile of books, learning the basic rules, regulations and practices of the railways, including sections K and M on train detection and detonator protection. We also had a basic training in the workings of a diesel locomotive.

Our first hands-on experience came two weeks into the course, when we were shown around locos 47069 and 25038, both of which were standing on Leicester depot. We practised coupling, using locos 25038 and 25180, and were also taught preparation (getting a loco ready) and disposal (shutting down a loco with all its lights and switches off).

Midway through our course we each had to go and book on at our respective depots. So at 8 a.m. on January 31st I arrived at Coalville to meet Craig and our instructor for the day. Our first trip was to Drakelow Power Station, just a stone's throw from my home. We rode to Coalfields Farm open-cast on two class 20s, which had been sent to bank a struggling 47343. Arriving back at Coalville depot I managed to get a ride back to Burton on another train.

But that experience was just a taster. The next day we were back in the classroom. My cab rides home became more frequent, but the weather took a definite turn for the worse. The whole network was almost at a standstill. One Thursday, instead of the usual Peak, a class 47 stormed into Leicester station with my homeward bound train. Snow was falling thickly and drifting in the bitter winds as I joined the driver for my almost regular cab ride. Once we hit 90 mph it looked as if we were running on a flat white road. None of the tracks were visible!

At Derby the problems continued. I boarded another class 47 for the last leg of my homeward journey. By now I had the confidence to introduce myself and invariably the crew would extend a warm welcome. Today's lot were Saltley men. Together we waited for the booked departure time - but it was two and a half hours later before we pulled out! Quite apart from the awful weather, I learned that four platelayers had lost their lives whilst clearing snow from points. There were other problems too: no class 56s were available due to an engineers' dispute. As part of their action they were refusing to undertake refuelling and watering work.

An actual footplate activity at the time was a trip from Nottingham to Cotgrave Colliery where we'd load up with coal for a trip to Ratcliffe Power Station. We returned then, light engine, to Toton MPD. (This particular day we were accompanied by a Toton instructor, Don Tennant.). We also took several supervised trips to Luton or St Pancras. I greatly enjoyed these passenger turns, especially in the days of the signal box and semaphore.

By now we'd reached the end of February. We split our time between Leicester and Coalville. One day we'd be racing up and down the Midland main line, the next on a more sober trip to Rugeley Power Station.

I had two worries to contend with. First and foremost, would I pass the course? But if I did, what was I to do about my own transport? I'd thought about moving into lodgings nearer to the Coalville depot, but was talked out of it by my parents. Instead I decided to do what I'd said at my interview: get a motorbike. I visited a showroom to choose one, and after I'd signed the paperwork the shop owner told me I could pick up my new machine on Saturday 24th February.

I'd never even ridden one before and with only two days to learn I was thrown in at the deep end. The man at the shop had promised to give me some lessons, but after only ten minutes he lost his patience with me and suggested I push it round to Anglesey Road 'rec for a practice. It seemed hopeless. How could I teach myself in such a short time? I'd end up killing myself or at the very least be hobbling around on crutches!

Help came in the shape of an old mate - one of the guards at Derby - who agreed to give me some tuition. What patience the man had! After the lesson I finally headed for home on my new bike, but I didn't feel at all happy about a trip on main roads all the way to Coalville. Sensing my nervousness the guard offered to escort me.

We set off just after 6 a.m. on that cold and frosty Monday morning. I wasn't sure if the butterflies in my stomach were from being out on the open road, or first day nerves about my new job. After thanking him for his kindness and assuring him I'd be alright he left me to book on for my first day at Coalville.

Our first day was spent with engine and brake, off the shed to Drakelow to pick up a train of 24-ton conventional wagons for Donisthorpe and Measham. Happily we trip-worked up and down all day before getting a lift back on a pair of class 20s.

The second day was the next hurdle. Craig and I were in front of the inspector, a Derby man by the name of George Hibbert, affectionately known as Skippy from his habit of tutting. We answered all his questions on the different aspects of our job. Then he watched as we coupled and uncoupled two class 20s on shed side. Without so much as a smile he said: 'Well done, you're through. You're drivers assistants.'

A quick handshake and that was it. We were thrilled, but one of our instructors, ex-Burton driver Ray Leer, soon brought us back to earth.

'Now you can start earning your wages,' he said.

6: Getting Started

My first week at Coalville was spent with the 08.00 ferry set crew. This job involved taking locos to other depots for fuel and water, as Coalville didn't have a fuelling point of its own. Nor did it have any fitters, so locos had to be taken elsewhere for sandbox filling or light maintenance work, usually to Leicester, Toton or Burton. I was no stranger to any of these places, but my visit to Burton seemed especially significant: I was now just like the young chap I'd envied that day on Moor Street Bridge. Or was I? My grade was Relief Drivers' Assistant - not even a proper second man - so maybe I had some way to go before I got too confident!

The driver I accompanied on these trips was an ex-Burton man and my best friend's dad, so we got on well from the start. He also offered me a lift in his car the next day - a kindness that he extended for several years whenever we were booked on together.

By the end of my first week, with no other second man available, I was asked to begin in the role. My first drive took place straight away, dragging 56050 with 08623. All in all a very progressive week.

The next week I spent second manning the 'Rugeleys' - coal wagons for the power station, but due to the continuing bad weather the coal kept freezing up in the wagons. I also learned the ground frame so as to help the guard whilst running round.

The first negative thing happened a few weeks later. I'd had some trouble with my motorbike so I went down to Burton shed to have a ride up to Coalville with the ferry. To my dismay there were no locos on. I waited a couple of hours, but to no avail. I'd have to find some other way of getting to work. I needed to book on time at 21.32 for a trip working to Willington Power Station. Once there we'd also be required to shunt the sidings, which were very big. The only option was to get a taxi. It cost me six pounds - quite a sum in those days. The lady cabbie said that she felt awful about charging me so much - but she never let me off any! I had to put it down to experience, but at least I made it to work on time. The train crew supervisor pointed to two class 20s and a brake van which stood waiting on goods road 2.

'There's your nags, Tony. Go and get on board. The driver'll be out shortly.'

Nodding timidly I did just that. Seconds later the cab door swung open and an irate-looking driver glared at me.

'What are you doing here? What do you want?'

'I'm your mate,' I explained in a shaky voice.

'I don't want you with me,' he said. 'And what's more, I'll get rid of you.'

With that he slammed the door and made his way back to the foreman's office. I was shocked. Whatever had I done to offend him? Open-mouthed, I watched the driver and the TCS shouting at each other, jabbing their fingers towards me and at each other. Eventually the driver stormed out of the office and made his way back to me. As he climbed up into the cab I braced myself for round two of his abuse. But he seemed to have calmed down a little.

'I don't want a young lad like you,' he explained. 'I want a passed man. It's my first turn back on the mainline. I've been medically restricted for the past two years.'

But there was no one but me available. I sensed he was coming round to the idea of taking me, but he wasn't happy about it and continued to be rather gruff with me.

'I'll have to take you then, if there's no one else. Go and check the fuel and water.'

When I told him I didn't know where they were he had kittens! As you can imagine, we were in for a long night.

Over the next few weeks, as I got to know that driver a bit better, I discovered he wasn't the old fuddy-duddy I'd taken him for. In fact we were destined to have some really pleasant shifts together in the coming months.

Getting to know the other second men was much easier. They were a friendly bunch, but some had a habit of asking you to swap shifts. All well and good, if done fairly, but I soon found myself wondering why I seemed to be getting all the bad jobs. I made my mind up from then on, that I'd only swap if it suited me or someone was genuinely desperate. Otherwise, a polite refusal was my policy.

But the drivers turned out to be not so hard-going as I'd feared. The ones who had worked at Burton soon got to know that I was Charlie Buckley's nephew - which made it a lot easier for them to accept me. Charlie was a likeable rogue with a taste for ale - though this might be a description of most railwaymen! The decent drivers would acknowledge me in the mess room, and I gradually got to know them all by second manning them, or through cadging a lift to work as I sometimes did.

One of the most unusual jobs came one Saturday morning. Snow had been falling all of Friday night and strong winds were sweeping it up into high drifts. So we were instructed to go off shed with a Class 47 and run up and down several times between Coalville and Moira to try and stop the build-up of snow in Coleorton Cutting. On the first run we burst through a wall of snow 9 feet high - quite an experience!

For saying that Coalville was only a small depot we had a good variety of work. We took coal to Rugeley and Drakelow power stations, and sometimes Ratcliffe. Landor Street Junction with trains bound for Didcot, Another well-trodden route for us was Wellingborough. The trains we took there were for West Drayton and Hayes & Harlington, but quite often we'd ferry locos to this location. Crewe, Derby and Nottingham were also thrown in. Certain drivers had specialised routes on their cards, like Barrow Hill and Northampton.

By mid-summer I was beginning to realise what a mixed bag of men we had at Coalville. Most were good conscientious railwaymen, but that was about the only thing they did have in common. Some chose to go about their day in a responsible professional manner, while others were far more laid back. They didn't seem to worry about the job as much as the older chaps and took the job of train driving very much in their stride. These were the ones who were most fun to be with, for us younger men anyway.

One cold autumn morning found me booking on for the 03.30 Rugeley. Not the best of times, but still a job in the link that required a second man. Today that second man was me. Checking the roster, I already knew who my driver and guard would be. Both were decent, so I had no worries on that score. We left the holding sidings at around 04.00 and ran light engine to Overseal Sidings. The guard went back to couple us to our train, then walked back to inspect and brake test it. Once he got back, we whistled the 'bobby' (signalman) in Moira West Box to let him know we were ready. The semaphore protecting the branch jerked up and we departed. I was still puzzled at the mysterious box the guard had carried into the back cab, but once underway I quickly forgot about it.

We came to a stand just north of Rugeley Trent Valley and began to set back onto a run round road. Then, with the operation of two ground frames, we ran round and began our climb towards Brereton signal box on the outskirts of Cannock Chase. After going over the signals we set back into the power station complex which was quite a distance. (The banner repeater forewarned us that the signal to which it repeated stood at danger.)

The driver desperately needed the toilet and he told me to go on the phone and ask the control room to have us down to the next signal, opposite the coal bunker where all the facilities were. The signalman told us he would pull off all the way down for us now so we carried on. The next move required us to set back a good half mile beyond the bunker and to draw up into one of the two unloading roads.

'Will you be alright to back it down and draw back up, Tony?' asked the driver.

I had barely six months experience and had never yet driven a loaded train. But I'd watched other drivers many times and knew their techniques. We wouldn't be going fast anyway, so I told him I could do it. The guard promised to keep an eye on me, so with that the driver got down and rushed off at breakneck speed to the loo!

We crept down behind the dolly and began to draw towards the bunker. As we approached the signal a figure came out of the station building running as fast as he could.

'What's up with him?' said the guard.

'Must be something wrong,' I said.

Wrong? We had a 17-year old driving a loaded train. The guard's mystery box was full of racing pigeons. The coffee on the hotplate had been laced with rum to keep the chill at bay. A fry-up was sizzling away on the same hot plate. And pop songs were blasting from our radio.

We stopped at the bunker signal. The driver climbed in, gasping for breath.

'Quick, put the mash can and the pigeons in the engine room. Out of the seat, Tony, and switch that flippin' radio off. Bloody hell, I can't be doing with this at this hour.'

The guard moved the fry-up and coffee can out of sight as ordered but was reluctant to put his prize pigeons in the same noisy fume-filled environment.

'No, I ain't putting them in there, it's full of ruddy diesel fumes. What the heck's the matter anyway?'

'Look, just do it. There's a loco inspector from Bescot down here checking driver's slips.'

With a gulp the guard shoved his birds into the engine room and shut the door. The driver - who I shall call Mabs - told us what had happened. After visiting the toilet, he went upstairs to take the coal consist to the control room and passed a man in an orange safety vest. Mabs asked the controller who the man was and had been told.

Barely had he got the story out when the said inspector was walking towards us and climbing up into the cab. After looking around and checking our documentation he seemed satisfied that all was well. We started to relax - apart from the guard that is, who kept looking anxiously towards the engine room. But the inspector was in no hurry to go and spent a good twenty minutes chatting to us before dismounting from the cab.

As soon as he'd gone we opened the engine-room door and rescued the poor birds. They seemed OK to me, and the guard seemed relieved. But what would a pigeon look like if it wasn't OK? The basket lid was lifted up for them and they took to the air with a great flapping of wings. Yet as they flew higher we could see they were all over the place as if drunk.

'It's the fumes,' said the guard.

He watched them anxiously as they fluttered to and fro. But after two laps around the power station's cooling towers they straightened out and headed towards Cannock.
'It's that way you clots!' the guard yelled, pointing eastwards.

But as the dawn sky lightened the dots carried on ever westwards. We watched helplessly. The 'cats eye' signal came off, so we climbed back on board our train and began to discharge our coal.

The next day the guard told us that the pigeons had eventually all found their way home, none the worse for their drunken adventure.

That same week, on the very same job with the very same crew, we witnessed a phenomenon. After leaving Overseal we dropped down the branch through Gresley Tunnel and on towards Coton Park. The morning was pitch black with heavy rain and our tired eyes peered into the inky beyond, each of us absorbed in our own thoughts. All of a sudden the whole sky erupted into a blue mass. It lasted for about five seconds and it was as if we were looking at the sky of a summer's day.

'What the...??' was the only sound I heard, uttered from somewhere in the cab.

Then, just as suddenly, it was dark again. Just as we were getting over the initial shock and discuss what it might be it happened again. And a third time. The last time I looked across at my companions and saw how the light had lit up their faces. We waited for another one, but it never came.

'That wasn't lightning, it hung in the sky too long.'

'I don't like to say it,' said Mabs, 'it could be a train crash on the Trent Valley line.'

The Trent Valley line ran parallel to our direction, about 25 miles the other side of the Sinai hills on the west side of Burton. The guard was of the opinion that an aeroplane had come down. My own conclusion was more sinister: with the cold war still in full swing I thought we were witnessing the start of a nuclear war.

We stopped at Branston to let a parcels train by and I was told to ask the signalman in the Derby power box if anything untoward had happened. All was well, as far he knew. Again I asked the signalman in the Colwich box, but he'd not heard of anything.

Over the next few weeks many people attempted to explain what we'd seen, but to this day I have never found a convincing theory.

58030 stands outside Desford Colliery box on a snowy day. Photo: Karl Brailsford.

7: Done Up Like A Dog's Dinner!

New Uniforms
Now in Stores!

Coalville's storeroom was housed in an old building attached to the big goods shed across the yard from our booking-on point. I'd been in it on my first day at the depot when Jack Johnson, the chap in charge, took me across to issue me with a hand-lamp, smock, coupling gloves and tin of Swarfega. The stores seemed old worldly, with shelves for brake-van side and tail-lights, shunting poles and brake sticks, Bardic hand-lamps and long smocks. Plus assorted ledgers and a whole range of stationery for the clerks and train crew supervisors.

'Blimey,' I said. 'There's some stuff in here! I bet you've even got an old driver or two from the steam days.'

'Yes,' he teased back, 'you'll find a couple in that corner there. Did you want them in bib and braces?'

As soon as the notice went up a gang of us turned up for our uniforms. The cardboard boxes were stacked ten high and a fair few across. Jack handed them over one by one as we signed our stores card. As I'd finished my shift all I had to do was secure the box on the back of my motorbike and head for home.

Next morning I opened the box and got ready for work. It seemed strange to be putting on a uniform - though it wasn't that long since I'd been wearing one for school! The jacket was the same design as a driver's, but with silver buttons instead of gold ones. It was also made of inferior material. The trousers were awful and, like many blokes before me, I suffered a nasty rash on the legs. The trousers felt better when your skin got used to them and they'd had a wash or two. But nearly everyone hated them. Some blokes reckoned they were woven from fibreglass, while others maintained that BR had bought a job lot of old army blankets and had them cut and sewn into trousers.

The slip-over vest jacket was more useful. The greatcoat was long and thick and ideal in cold weather. In rain though it was useless: the water just soaked in and added to the misery! Most men's favourite was the light blue smock, similar to those worn in steam days. With two deep waist pockets and a breast pocket for documents and diary they were ideal and though officially 'summer issue', most Coalville blokes wore them all year round.

My first day in uniform had arrived. As I walked from the bike sheds I began to worry about what the other blokes would say. Like most people who have to wear a uniform, I was wondering how people would judge me. Would it suit me - or would I look like a sack of spuds?

With that thought I slipped through the lobby and into the locker room. No one would have noticed anything yet as my Belstaff motorbike jacket covered all. Stashing the bike gear in my locker I crept quietly back into the lobby. By now I'd convinced myself that I was over-reacting. Surely no one would even notice! But I was wrong, as I soon found out when a fellow second-man joined me at the roster board.

'Bloody hell - I didn't recognise you.'

I turned pink and nodded a greeting before turning back to the noticeboard. I wasn't looking at anything in particular - I was just anxious to avoid scrutiny. Suddenly a motley group came out of the mess room and headed towards the TCS office.

'Hey, look at Gregory!' someone shouted. 'He's done up like a dog's dinner.'

Hooting with laughter they went on their way. That had really unnerved me and I spent another hour in the lobby before I could pluck up courage to enter the mess room.

The two top tables were full of drivers, guards and shunters. Two card schools were in progress and the place was noisy and boisterous. I saw some of the younger second men at one of the back tables, so after taking a deep breath I headed towards them. Keep looking forward, I told myself, don't turn left. But it had gone very quiet. I'd just about reached the table when all at once a loud cheer went up. People were stamping their feet and wolf whistles pierced the air. All the second men started laughing. I felt the blood rush to my face. I wanted the ground to open up and swallow me.

But I sat down. After a while the guffaws turned to chuckles and gradually died away. The joke quickly ran its course. As I joined in the chat, I began to feel a bit better. That was the only bit of leg pulling I endured over my uniform. Over the years I've seen many other poor devils go through it - and sometimes took part in it myself. But as far as Coalville was concerned it seemed as if the blokes were used to me and I'd had my initiation. I proudly pinned on my ASLEF badge to my lapel and became one of the lads.

That year saw the beginning of the rout of the branch link. These old boys - all of them over sixty - had done their bit and been put out to grass, left with just the local trip work. Most were decent chaps, but there were a few old devils who didn't like young hands at all. We didn't get to work with them that often, but when you did it was either a good week or a miserable one. Thankfully the bad weeks were rare.

A major change was about to take place, one that would greatly affect us all in the coming months and years. In that year's general election Margaret Thatcher romped home with a landslide victory. A lot of people were happy with Mrs T's victory, but many were devastated. In the early hours of the morning I witnessed my parents crying over the outcome.

Earlier on that Election Day I was to have my first proper drive on the main line. Around 8 p.m. on a lovely sunny evening driver Mick Riley and I left Burton MPD with two class 20s. Crossing Leicester Junction we accelerated away past the back gardens of Anglesey Road.

'Have you had a drive yet Tony?' Mick asked.

'Only on shed and in the power station.'

'Come and sit here if you want,' he said, vacating the driver's seat and motioning me across.

I didn't need asking twice. Secondmen - most of us anyway - desperately wanted to be in that seat. With some of us it was almost an obsession and it was with great pride that I drove the class 20s back. We put the locos on shedside and shut the engines down. It may have been only two Class 20s up a branch line, but it had been a great experience and I thanked Mick for giving me the opportunity.

At 11 p.m. we got the 'right away' home, but because of bike trouble I would have to ride back home on a Drakelow or something. An ex-Burton driver, Jack Sharpe, approached me.

'You after a lift home, Tony? We're taking five engines back down to Burton shortly. Do you want to come with us?'

'Certainly, Jack,' I replied. 'If you don't mind.'

At 11.30 we squealed off from the holding sidings with Jack's mate, Pat, in the driver's seat. As we left Coalville and headed down the dark branch, the only lights visible were the fault and markers. I stood with my arms behind my back, holding the parking brake wheel to balance myself. Jack's voice broke the silence.

'Have you driven an engine yet Tony?'

'Yes, I had my first go tonight with Mick Riley.'

'Right, Pat, shall we give him a go with all this weight on?'

Due to the darkness I couldn't see the evil glint that was probably in his eye!

'Why not?' agreed Pat.

Climbing into his seat I soon saw the downside of driving. My palms were sweating as the weight kept pushing me above maximum speed for the branch. In the darkness I couldn't even see where we were or what speed restrictions were in force. It was a trip of terror! And, I realised, another kind of initiation. No matter how many times I asked to get out they just kept saying 'It's alright, Tony, you'll soon get the hang of it.'

By the time we reached the iron bridge I was a quivering wreck. Thanking them both I vacated the driver's seat and got off. It was just after midnight as I walked up the bank and across the bridge. The lonely tail-light of the rear loco disappeared into the darkness. I was relieved to be off it, but all in all I felt rather pleased with the day's experiences and smiled to myself in the cold night air.

8: Boffins and Loco Tales

The traction at Coalville varied only slightly. It was mainly pairs of Class 20s and single Class 47s, plus a few of the new Class 56s. We were given the newest members of the class - probably because the locations we went to and the physical state of the branch with its mining subsidence would really put the locos through their paces. These brand-new freshly-painted locos were a pleasure to ride on. The cabs smelled clean and the main engine and smaller motors all had a nice precise sound to them.

The only drawback was the boffins from the Railway Technical Centre in Derby who often accompanied them. Their meters and cases full of testing equipment were all over the cab and proved a real nuisance. But we had no choice but to grin and bear it!

One morning, on an early 'Rugeley', one boffin rode with us to test the air-conditioning unit below the cab floor. An arrogant man, he jumped into my seat as soon as I got down at Overseal to extinguish the tail-lights. And there he sat all the way to Rugeley. I could tell that my mate was seething and he was quick to make his views known.

'May as well go and get your feet up with the guard, Tony. It doesn't look like he's going to shift himself.'

The boffin gave us a quick look and carried on staring out of the window. I took my mate's advice and went down to the guard. My mate told me later that the man hadn't done anything except sit there.

We'd heard on the grapevine that a Class 56 - 56036 - had been painted with an experimental livery. Two days later we were able to see for ourselves when it turned up on shed. Still in BR blue it now had extra large number and logo. Its roof had been decked out in silver and both cabs painted wrap-around yellow.

'That won't stop like that for long,' said one of the old hands as he gave it the once-over.

Too right! The front was soon covered in dead flies and the roof and sides soiled with coal-dust and grime from the collieries and power stations we visited. It even had stains from its own exhaust fumes!

One bright Saturday morning found me on the 06.00 ferry with driver Jack Sharpe.

'We've got to take that 56036 to Burton for fuel water and hydrostat,' he told me. 'It's on the dock road.'

Once at Burton, fitter Jack Fern set about the maintenance work while we refreshed ourselves with sandwiches and a cup of tea.

'That's a bit of a celebrity engine, eh Tony?' said Jack, pointing with his sandwich. 'Shall we clean it when we've finished our grub?'

56036 arrives at Rawdon photographed in 1979. Photo: John Tuffs.

We found two of the long-handled brushes usually used for windows and two buckets for some water. Jack asked the fitter if he had anything special that would help us get rid of the grime and deceased flies. The fitter disappeared into the stores and emerged a moment later with a plastic container.

'This is what we use in the screen washers. It's acid-based, mind, so don't get using too much of it!'

With that he walked off to finish his jobs. Jack put a liberal amount of the stuff in each bucket and topped up with hot soapy water.

'Right Tony, you start this end and I'll start the other. Hopefully we'll meet up somewhere near the middle.'

With gusto I set about scrubbing up the front end and was pleased to see all the dead flies running away in a torrent of suds. As I carried on I noticed that the water in my bucket was tinged with yellow, only pale at first, but gradually deepening, so that a stream of intense yellow was soon running down into the pit. Looking up I was horrified to see that a pink undercoat had replaced the once yellow cab front!

'Right, Tony, that's enough,' said Jack. The same thing had happened at his end too. 'Chuck the water away. The fitter's finished with us, so let's get going.'

And so I drove the odd-looking engine back to Coalville. Neither of us actually mentioned the incident on the way. We berthed the loco on No.1 road and went home.

Sunday evening saw 56036 leave with the ferry set, probably en route for Doncaster. It was back within a few weeks, restored to its original condition. The loco was a firm favourite with at least one of ours TCSs. He rewarded us for allowing him to accompany it when another driver and I took it to Nuneaton depot open day on a Friday evening, fetching it back the following Monday. (what reward?)

Whilst on the subject of individual locos, a certain Class 47 - number 47281 - springs to mind. I had three incidents on her in two weeks...

The first was in Mantle Lane Sidings. We were attached to our train awaiting our guard's return from doing a brake test. The driver told me to put on the hot-plate so we could have our first mash prior to departure. We'd filled our cans with boiling water in the mess room before leaving so the water needed just a few minutes to re-boil. I switched the hot-plate to maximum I expected the element to be glowing within minutes. To my surprise it was still cold. I tried the switch at all positions, holding my hand near to check for heat.

'Is there a problem?' asked my mate.

'Must be,' I said. 'I've tried it all ways but there's no heat at all.'

'You're a jinx, Tony!' he joked. 'I've a good idea what it is. Come on, I'll show you.'

I followed him down to the rear cab and we entered the engine room No.2 end. This was the area that used to house the boiler, but it had been taken out and replaced by a large metal weight. Beyond this, just inside the engine room, were two cabinets of assorted switches, fuses and circuit-breakers. He got out his T-key to open the Perspex door.

Jinxed loco 47281 up to its tricks in 1978 after joining the branch from the Birmingham Curve. Photo: the late Bert Wynn.

'There's your problem,' he said. 'The fuse has gone. Now there's a proper way to do this - just watch. Shut the engine down first of all and I'll get the spare fuses.'

I did as asked and a moment later he was back with the fuses. They were quite large - the size of pepperpots - and held in place by two large bolts with a square T-key head. But our culprit turned out to be just a 32-amp plug-in one, one of four, the others being two 60-amp heater fuses for 1 and 2 cabs and the redundant boiler fuse, also 60-amp. He unplugged the blown one and handed it to me before fitting the new one. It wasn't easy to do, as it was dark in there and we had to use hand-lamps to see by. Suddenly there was a loud bang and a white flash like a hundred camera flashes going off at once. A terrified yelp rang out - then silence.

'Are you alright?' I called anxiously.

'Yes, but I've just realised - we should have taken the battery isolating switch out too!'

'I don't know about these things,' I said. 'But I'm sure I saw your skeleton just then!'

The four fuses had fused together in their housing, so that put paid to our heating too. Luckily the weather was mild, so it was bearable. But there'd be no hot drinks for us for the rest of our shift.

Later that week we found ourselves on 47281 again. She'd been for repairs and was as good as new - or so we thought. We'd been to Drakelow and were passing through the long signal-less section between Moira and Coalville when she suddenly shut down. We were able to coast as far as the road bridge at the old Ashby station, but no amount of coaxing would get her started. We'd completely failed. Mabs sent me back to put down full detonator protection whilst the guard used a public phone box to arrange assistance.

A week later I had her yet again, this time with my mate Charlie Farren. It was the 18.00 ferry, which left the holding sidings with five engines, the leading one being the jinxed 47281. Everything was fine until we reached Swadlincote Junction. Yet again the loco just shut down on us. Confident that the other engines in the set were maintaining the air brake, Charlie let it run on to Burton.

'Let's hope Derby box are on their toes and there's nothing about,' he said.

A single yellow at Branston said the opposite and we had to slow. We were just preparing to stop at the exit signal off the branch when it came off with the indicator showing a 'G' for goods line.

'That's good,' said Charlie. 'They're having us. I'll drop you off behind the dolly on the bridge. Tell our riders to stop me when we're over and drag us back onto the shed.'

Once on shed the fitters went over all five of the locos, the jinx one being last. Their verdict was that for some reason - probably an electrical fault - the fire extinguisher in the engine room had gone off on its own. And so 47281 was detached and would now be sent to Toton for repairs. The engine room would also have to be cleaned and all the bottles refilled.

That was my last association with 47281 for many years and, ironically, I wrote some of these memoirs whilst on board her fifteen years later.

47281 and the branch didn't seem to mix. She was also involved in the derailment of three MGR wagons on the Birmingham Curve back in 1978.

Around the same time I was to be on another jinxed 47, the better known 47299. This loco has a more sinister history, but during my shift on her I banged my knee on the desk, dropped and lost my desk key in the engine room, then slipped down the hand rail landing heavily. I was glad to get off it!

Busy scene at Moira with a trio of class 58s. Photo: John Oldershaw

9: Burton Loco and Other Stories

Burton loco (or fuelling point as it became in 1975) was finally closed in 1982, bringing to a close another chapter in the town's railway history.

By mid-1979 I was second-manning locos off and on there. An ex Burton driver - Bill Clemson - stayed on after 1975 to attend to engine movements and preparing and disposing of locos. We second men would assist the fitters by putting fuel and water pipes on and filling loco sandboxes, which we did by means of a specially-adapted can with a long thick spout. Our assistance was greatly appreciated by the two regular fitters and their mates - on one shift the Fern brothers Jack and George and the other shift Barry and Maurice. Some second men would help by changing the air filters on the Class 56s, but it was such a filthy job that most of us steered well clear!

One day, whilst putting the fuel pipe on I witnessed a second man get sprayed with diesel fuel. The non-return valve had become unseated and he was drenched from head to toe. Diesel fuel is horrible stuff when in contact with the skin, so I really felt for the poor devil as he hosed himself down and did his best to soap it off. When he'd got off as much as he could he donned an old pair of overalls and was taken straight back to Coalville. A new uniform arrived for him within a week.

As the weeks went on I booked on and off at Burton quite often, typically with Charlie Farren who got the 08.00 ferry every three weeks. Quite often there were locos that had been left overnight and were required to go back to Coalville. The TCS would phone up Charlie to tell him to go straight down to the loco. He would then pick me up and we would fetch the engines. This also happened with the 18.00 ferry, though not as often.

Another reason many of us would sign at Burton was for Sunday ballast trains. They had numerous Burton drivers to use. These would sometimes double up. A few second and passed men who lived locally would also be asked, along with a number of guards, so when these engineers' trains were required in the Burton area we were used.

I booked on at Burton many times, sometimes as many as three sets of us. At the end the locos were stabled back onto the depot awaiting ferrying up the branch. On a couple of occasions, due to severe weather, they allowed us to book on there and a light engine would run down the branch to pick as many as a dozen of us up. So even though I can never class myself as a Burton man, I can say that I've booked on there many times.

At Christmas we would leave all of our allocation of locos on there, then fetch them back after New Year. I sometimes wondered why they ever shut the place. Many early days were had taking locos down, then going straight home. Thinking back to my childhood, at the stroke of midnight New Year's Eve the town's church bells were joined by diesel horns from the loco, all in loud chorus to celebrate the new year.

One morning, as we waited for our engines to be done, a class 50 loco came onto the depot. It was to be the first of many over the coming weeks. The reason was that Saltley men had started training on them. They would run up to Burton light engine, the crew would have their grub, then go back sharing the driving. That first day, still being a bit of an enthusiast and with a liking for that class I stood there admiring it. A voice roared out behind me in a strong West Midlands accent.

'Haven't you seen a 50 before then? They're not much different to another engine. But do us a favour and take it round to the departure road. And swap the lights round while you're about it, there's a good lad. We're having our grub now.'

Thrilled to bits, I did as I was asked - the one and only time I've ever driven a Class 50 and on my local depot too.

1975 marked the 150th anniversary of the Stockton & Darlington Railway. As many as fourteen steam engines were supposed to be coming through Burton on their way to the celebrations. A group of us spent the night on the roof of a hut opposite the sheds. But no steamers came through and by 6 a.m. we sat surrounded by frost. Seeing us there, cold and tired, a driver on duty took pity on us and brought over a steaming can of hot tea. It soon brought us back to life.

'I've been watching you daft buggers all night,' he chortled. 'I bet you're freezing.'

It turned out that we'd been wasting our time - the steamers were all coming through during the day!

We found out later that the driver's name was Jack Dockerty, a pleasant little chap who had once been in a bad train crash in Wolverhampton when his driver was burned to death.

One of the Coalville TCSs turned out to be Ronnie Harrison, an ex-Burton supervisor who I remembered from my old spotting days. He'd stuck in my mind because of something he had done to me...

A Clayton loco had turned up on the branch one Sunday afternoon. No one knew what it was doing there, but we saw it go into the loco. Never having seen such an exotic sight before we left my Auntie's house and headed for the depot. By the time we got there the Clayton was stabled and shut down. Its crew were walking over the boards towards a car. Slinging our bikes against the wall of the office, we walked up onto the yard for a better look. At this time the depot was still manned but no foreman had been on duty for weeks and we thought we'd be OK. After a good nosey round the engine we walked back to our bikes. To our horror we saw they had been padlocked to a large cast-iron drainpipe. We walked round the office building several times shouting plaintively.

'Excuse me, is anyone inside?'

Nothing stirred. All the doors were locked. And so we had no other option but to walk four miles home to fetch our parents. They had to phone my uncle to take us back down to the depot to try and retrieve our bikes. No one was exactly pleased! A little man emerged from the shed office and words were exchanged. We had to admit that we were in the wrong for trespassing, so after a ticking off our bikes were handed back.

Now, nearly five years later, I booked on and here he was that very same little man again...

'I recognised you straight away,' he said with a grin.

He made no reference to the misery he'd put us through that day and I thought that it was about time I took revenge...

On the TCS's desk were four telephones. I swapped around all the handsets so when one rang he had to pick up at least three before getting the right one!

By now I was courting a Burton girl and would often call at her house when I arrived in Burton on the 18.00 ferry. I only had till 11 o'clock though, as that was the time we headed back. Once we walked back to the loco hand in hand.

'Come on Tony, the dolly's off!' the driver shouted impatiently.

After a quick goodnight kiss, I jumped on to the waiting locos and was off.

One Sunday evening Charlie Farren, myself and two riders booked on for the 23.59 ferry, a full set of five locos to be taken for fuel, water and repairs. Joining Leicester Junction opposite the loco we noticed that there were four more engines to go back. Now Charlie liked to get everything finished early and whoever was on with him always mucked in so we could get the locos back a.s.a.p. As we positioned the first loco in the wind tunnel Jack came up.

'You're going to be late tonight, Chas,' he said with a malicious grin. 'It looks like two trips. Them four need to go back up as well.'

'Late?' said Charlie. 'Oh no we won't - we'll take the lot.'

We all looked at each other.

'You're not serious!' said Jack. 'You know five's the maximum.'

Action stations! The young riders went across to get the four locos ready, whilst the fitters and us got our five done. After some shunting we joined our engine which was right up on the old neck opposite Anglesey Rec. The last loco stood at the departure dolly. Steadily we began to roll off the shed and came to a stand behind the dolly on the bridge. The riders said afterwards that they were opposite the north end of the platform when we finally stopped. We reached Coalville safely but had about two hours of shunting due to the amount and length of the engines. The signalman in Mantle Lane box was pulling out his hair as he pulled off his signals for all the different moves.

As we made our way home I said to Charlie:

'The only thing that worried me was - '

'I know what you're going to say,' he interrupted. 'The viaduct and the weight. It made me think too!'

A few weeks previously I'd been with Charlie on a Sunday ballast (Engineer's track maintenance train). We were taken by taxi to the Cadley Hill branch adjacent to the colliery screens. It was a pleasant sunny afternoon as we relieved the day men and they went back in our taxi. We tried to get as comfortable as possible, but on Class 20s that wasn't so easy! We made a few more moves, dropping off stone, then waited until required again. From the west a huge black cloud crept towards us. There must have been a couple of dozen P-way men working on the line when all of a sudden the heavens opened up. The men scattered, taking shelter in vans, in the plough brake or under the A444 road bridge. At the side of the line was an old concrete fogman's hut, half leaning due to subsidence, into which one of the platelayers dived. Seconds later, much to my surprise, he came dashing out in a panic and joined his mates under the road bridge.

Eventually the rain abated and they all got back to work. A couple of hours later the men started to put away their equipment and climbed into their mess truck. The person-in-charge came up and gave us the necessary paperwork.

'You're going forward to Chad Sidings with this lot, mate.'

'Nasty bit of weather you had just now,' said Charlie.

'Yes, it was. But the lads soon scattered.'

'Did you see that one jump out of the old fogman's hut?' I asked.

'He came up to me in a right state,' the head ganger said. 'He'd gone in the place and half lay down on the sloping side. He'd seen a movement in front of his boots, then when his eyes got used to the dark he saw what it was - a bloody snake wavering from side to side!'

We all laughed...until we began to think what it must have been like. We fell silent then until with a throaty cough the PIC gave us permission to leave.

There have always been snakes round the area. The woods around Drakelow used to have signs nailed to the trees: DANGER! BEWARE OF SNAKES. I grew up around those woods and Dad would always be telling me to be careful, though he said if I ever did come across one I should bring it home for a family pet.

That chance arose one Sunday morning when my mates and I found one slithering about in the young green corn. Laying claim to it, I managed to get it coiled around a long stick and set off home with my prize. As Dad came out I proudly showed him our new pet.

'That's an adder,' he said, trying to stay calm. 'You've brought home an adder. Look at the diamond pattern.'

We dropped it gently into a large sweet jar and tried to tempt it with some morsels of meat. But it soon lost patience and toppled the jar over, its fangs just inches from my head. Then it slithered across the path and entwined itself around the base of a lilac tree. Mum reckoned that our neighbours had threatened to leave the street if it wasn't caught soon. So the police had to be called to smoke it out and take it away. From then on I steered well clear of snakes!

Ironically I was on the last ferry set to go onto Burton loco. I say 'set' but it was one Class 47. Again my driver was Mick Riley. We'd signed on at 18.00 but weren't given the job until half past nine. We left the holding sidings and picked our way down the dark branch with me in the chair. Mick wanted to rush down for a last pint. This was an accepted practice in those days. Although the rulebook outlawed alcohol at work, no one seemed to bother as long as nothing went wrong. Most blokes were sensible and stuck to the rules, but one or two others weren't.

'Come on, Tony, hurry up or we won't get a pint!'

With that I pulled out all the stops. We burst into Gresley Tunnel, then out the other end. There were no headlights in those days, just dim markers. Suddenly, quick as a flash, someone hurled themself out of the way. Another dark figure shot forward for a second. There was a dull thud against the cab. My speedo showed 45 mph so we weren't speeding. Mick had seen better than me.

'Bloody hell, Tony. He was lucky. His dog's had it though.'

My stomach tightened. An animal lover myself I carried on towards Burton wondering sadly how the owner would be feeling. Mind you, it was a silly place to be walking a dog at night.

After a pick-me-up we left the Burton loco for the last time and ambled back up the branch, slowing down towards the spot where the accident had happened. There lay a beautiful collie dog. Shining our lamps we could see that it was beyond help, so we carried on back to Coalville. Burton loco and the dog were now both gone for good.

Towards the end of 1979, again on the 08.00 ferry, we were given the job of fetching Desford Colliery's shunters out. There was no longer any work for them and they were redundant. We used a class 08 shunter to trip them back to Coalville. They'd already been sold and were taken away on lorries.

Another second man started around that time. He let himself down badly a few months later at a wedding in Birmingham. Whilst making conversation with some of the wedding guests he told them - quite rightly - that he was on the footplate at Coalville. To colour his story though he told them he had been testing the APT (Advanced Passenger Train), which was at that time undergoing trials. Those in the group who knew little about railways were most impressed by the young man. Behind him though was another guest, a Saltley driver, who now stepped forward.

'So how long have Coalville men been testing APTs then?'

Once rumbled by one of his own profession the young man made his excuses and hurried off to another part of the room. But the poor devil wasn't going to get off so lightly. Saltley cabin often played host to Coalville men as they awaited empties from Didcot, and the story soon spread. Before long the poor chap had a new name - APT Smith.

Some of the young shunters based at Coalville were a bit lively. Some of the tricks they played were downright dangerous. On one occasion they raided the First Aid box and used some plasters to stick lengths of toilet paper to men's jackets and set them alight. They thought it was funny, but most of us considered it a step too far. Another time one of the shunters brought a crossbow to work and started taking pot shots at the mess room noticeboard. But this time they were warned in no uncertain terms to get the dangerous weapon off the premises or face the sack.

These shunters were big rough blokes who had a tendency to bully the younger second men. I thought that I might be an easy target, but it wasn't always easy to tell which ones they'd go for and which they'd leave alone. One day though they bit off more than they could chew. Heavy snow lay a foot deep in the yard and between shunting duties they amused themselves by snowballing passers-by in the street below Mantle Lane signalbox. More by luck than skill they hit one chap straight on the side of the head. The shunters were in hysterics. The man glared up at them, then walked on under the bridge. As they waited for another target the man suddenly appeared behind them. Striding across, he punched the biggest of the shunters squarely on the nose. The others thought twice about tackling him, so after giving them a piece of his mind he left. Justice had prevailed. The shunter picked himself up and tried to stem the blood from his damaged nose.

As my first year drew to a close one more incident happened.

I was on a ballast train with driver Raz Keen and guard Ivor Haskett, taking a train back to Sandiacre ballast sidings. We dropped off the guard and went over the dolly. Once it was off we began to set back. Ivor was my side, so I was relaying signals to the driver.

'We must be in the clear now. Is he still calling us?' asked Raz.

'Yes, he's still calling.'

Then there was a sudden surge and we stopped. Seconds later the guard's arms shot skywards.

'Whoaw, Raz, he's stopped us.'

Looking back for further signals I saw Ivor pick up his traps (equipment & food bag) and hurry along the train towards us. Panting heavily he climbed up into the cab.

'We've pushed them too far. There's three in the pond!'

To this day I'll never know if they actually went into the pond, but he certainly looked worried.

'Is the train secure?' he asked. 'It won't go anywhere will it?'

'Not on your life.'

'Well let's go, Tony. Go and bell out light engines to Coalville.'

And with that we left the sidings and nothing was heard about this incident again.

10: Settling Down

As I approached the end of my first year on the job everything seemed settled. I thought of myself as a small but essential cog in a large well-oiled machine. From the longest-serving driver to the youngest shunter the men of the branch were close in those days. Comradeship prevailed and wherever you went the atmosphere was friendly. Animosity over pay was, as yet, unknown and we all had to work overtime to make a decent wage. Most of the men were professional and this conscientiousness tended to rub off on us younger men. Resourcefulness in a crisis was another common virtue amongst railwaymen and I prided myself on being the same.

There were always a few who didn't give a hoot about the job, but they were rare. On the other hand some seemed almost obsessed. One particular yard inspector springs to mind. He'd gone home at 6 a.m. after a 12-hour shift, but couldn't sleep for the worrying about some wagons standing on 'A' road in Mantle Lane. It seemed they were in the way and needed to be shifted. And so at 8 o'clock, instead of being sound asleep, he was on the phone to the depot to see if they'd been moved.

I'd always lived near to the Leicester line. We'd moved house a few months after I started on the railway and so I was now even closer, just up the bank from the east arrival signal at Drakelow. I got into the habit of whistling my parents as I passed and gradually we evolved a recognised code to let them know what time I'd be back. On receiving my horn code Mum would give me two hours - one to get back to the depot and another one to get back to the house. It ensured that my dinner was always nice and hot when I got in! If I knew I would be longer then I wouldn't whistle at all. Our system worked well - until my mates started imitating my code as they passed by. One evening I got back to a very burnt meal. When I looked at it askance Mum told me she had heard my code four hours back and so had the dinner ready two hours after that.

'But I haven't been off the shed today,' I exclaimed.

'Well, someone whistled,' she insisted.

And so my code had to be regularly changed after that to stop similar tricks.

Night shifts have never been my favourite and I always seem to be running on only three cylinders. I once did six weeks of 12-hour nights. That was a real killer. They were all shed turns too. Yet some chaps actually prefer nights and will even swap shifts to get on them. They seem to function better and be more natural in the small hours.

22.00 shed wasn't a bad shift. Engines had to be got ready for various jobs: a set of engines for a tripper, the night ferry set of between one and five locos, a loco for the night Didcot, then the engines for the 01.25 Wellingborough. When those were done it would go quiet until the 03.30 Rugeley loco required preparation. After that had gone off it was time to sweep all the cabs out and check fuel and water levels. To me this time between 3 am and 4 am was the worst. I'd be totally whacked and just couldn't help my eyelids closing.

Of the three regular shed drivers, two of them - Alf Hough and Jack Manley - were ex Burton. The third, Harold Marlow, was a proper Coalville man. Unfortunately he had been dealt a cruel hand regarding deaths on the line and it affected him so much that he took premature retirement.

One night, whilst on shed with Alf, I went to prepare the Wellingborough class 20s. Alf was involved with his usual game of crash, so would ask his mate to do it. We didn't mind: it was all experience to us second men and we welcomed any chance to drive, especially on our own. A pair of Class 20s were booked for the job and were standing as usual at the stop block on the shedside road. They'd probably been there since the afternoon after shunting the Bardon Hill tanks. They were cold and the main air reservoir had leaked off. Had I known that, the situation that was about to happen may not have....

My plan was to take the parking brake off at the stop- block end, put the BIS (battery isolating switch) and lighting switch in, then start them up the opposite end. Once the main air reservoir was up the parking brake at the other end could be taken off.

But I never got that far...

As I took the first brake off the 20s began to roll down the gentle gradient. I was terrified. All I could imagine was them sailing off shed and gathering speed until they joined the main line at Burton and smashed into an oncoming train! Desperately I spun the wheel to put the brake on, but it made no difference. Without air in the system the controls were useless. In sheer desperation I jumped down and grabbed hold of the buffers, actually thinking I could stop 144 tons of locos. Not a chance! They pulled me along too.

And then, halfway between the block and the departure dolly, the 20s suddenly stopped and began to roll back. They stopped a second time, then continued to roll back. As fast as I could I slammed in the BISs and started the engines up. Only when the main air reservoir had built up did I relax.

Once I'd secured the locos I climbed down and headed for the cabin. If I expected sympathy I would have a long wait. Excitedly I told my story, but this was the railways and no one took much notice. Alf didn't even look up from his card game, but merely muttered.

'They won't go far, son. There's a kink in the rail so they'll stop there.'

And with that he carried on with his game.

*

Whilst on the subject of Wellingborough... One such job, on which I was second man, entailed a taxi to Leicester station to catch the last train down. Sometimes we came back with a train, other times just light engine. One night, as there was no train to work back, an old driver and I set out with two Class 20s. The Midland main line can be a dark featureless road at night and as the driver wasn't very chatty I began to nod off. No one on our job means to nod off, it just comes on you. One minute you're fine, then it's like lapsing into unconsciousness. Normally it's only for a few seconds and you're awake again.

I rubbed my eyes and looked across at the driver. His head nodded with the motion of the engine and I could see he was spark out too. I thought about waking him but then thought better of it. In those days we were all instilled with a certain respect for the old hand drivers. He probably knows what's going on I thought. The speedo read 60 mph, so that was OK. Then I checked the 'sunflower' or AWS indicator. If it showed yellow and black it would mean we had passed a restrictive aspect and I'd have to slam on the brakes. It was black, however, so we were running on greens. From then on I stayed awake and alert until he shook his head, looked at me, then went back to sleep.

A few weeks later I second-manned a driver who I didn't think of as very sociable. The driver's name was Jimmy Robinson, a tall big-boned chap and dedicated union man. He always looked me up and down with contempt - or so I thought. But as I later found out it was just his way and I was reading too much into it. Most second men kept a record of the drivers who let them drive and I was no exception. One second man, Roy Butcher, used to give them stars, but that was going too far in my book. My list had grown to twelve but I didn't think I'd be adding to it this night!

It was about midnight as we walked through the rain to our engine, climbed aboard and ambled off shed to fetch our Drakelow-bound train from the west end of Mantle Lane. I was preparing for a long night in dubious company, but suddenly Jimmy started chatting pleasantly. Some drivers were like that: silent and gloomy in the cabin, but quite different out on the main line. Mind you, some were the opposite.

As we unloaded the last few trucks, I began to think that it wouldn't be such a bad night after all. We drew up to the Stop board and the guard climbed down to uncouple. I gathered up my bag, coat and lamp and prepared to change ends. Jimmy sat back in his chair with his feet up. I couldn't help wondering what was going on. But Instead of asking him straight and jeopardising our new friendship, I decided to use tact.

'Do you want your bag and lamp passing down, Jim?'

'No, I'll stay here if it's alright with you, Tony. I've done my bit.'

'What, are you saying you want me to drive back, Jim?'

'Yes, if you like. You've driven before haven't you? I've got complete confidence in you, by what I've heard on the grapevine. See you later.'

With that he shut his eyes. Closing the door quietly so as not to disturb him I changed ends. Like a dog with two tails I climbed into the back cab. The guard climbed in through the other door. He stared at me as I keyed in and opened the brake valve.

'Where's Jim?' he asked.

'He's got his head down in the back cab. He's asked me to take us back.'

The guard shrugged. As long as someone was getting us back safely and into our beds he wasn't overly concerned. He gave me the tip to run round and I drove back as carefully as I could.

And so it had turned out to be a very different night to the one I'd expected - my first drive on the mainline unaccompanied by a driver. Not only that, but judging by his comment about the grapevine, I must have been making a good impression!

A class 56 stands at Drakelow Sidings awaiting examination as dusk falls on a windy evening.
Photo: Anthony Gregory.

11: Traction and a Bank Fire at Desford

By the end of my first year I was extremely happy with my lot. It was the job I'd always dreamt of. The only thing I'd have liked would have been more mixed traction work. For drivers and second men at depots like Derby and Saltley every day might be different. One day they'd be at the helm of a Class 45 or 50 speeding through beautiful countryside on an express; the next could bring the monotonous stop-start-stop business of a DMU; and the third day a heavy freight train that required different braking techniques.

I'd put in for Derby, just to experience this kind of variety, but after some thought I took the move out. I was happy where I was. With hindsight it's probably just as well: I was to enjoy just as many interesting and happy years on that Leicestershire branch line. The variety of work may have been limited - carting coal, stone or ferry sets about - but the job, the men and the attitudes were the same at every depot. Everyone was doing their bit, each one a small but essential cog that made the whole machine work.

But different types of traction did turn up from time to time, mostly on weekend engineering trains. Many's the time these would be headed by a Class 45, 25, 31 or 37, all normally strangers to Coalville crews. The drivers rostered on these jobs were men who had transferred from other depots and learnt these locos there. Our ex Burton men, for instance, who had brought with them huge traction experience and route knowledge. We also had former employees from Derby, Toton and Nottingham, so it meant that Coalville crews could be rostered on most forms of traction. So could we second men, because we weren't required to sign a road or traction.

Even though our duties as second men were limited, we were the drivers of tomorrow - so we were told - and had to be nurtured in the ways of footplate life. This meant booking on and off at all hours, eating our snap on the loco amid diesel fumes, being out for twelve hours or more at a time, never having a nice clean loo nearby. Some men grumbled a bit, but their whinges fell on deaf ears. It was the job we had chosen and these were the conditions that came with it. Most of us soon learned to take all these things in our stride.

On the subject of unavoidable overtime, the worst case I heard of was a crew who'd put in a continuous 24 hours. A Rugeley train had failed in the plant and after a while a crew and loco were mustered to go out and drag it back. But once there, the assisting loco failed too and so a third loco and crew had to be found. They were more successful, but by the time they'd completed the job the first crew had been on duty a whole 24 hours!

My longest time was 18 hours - still 'fresh on' according to one leg-pulling driver!

As I said before, our regular locos were Classes 20s, 47s and 56s. But during my time I've also worked on 45s, 25s, 31s and 37s. Not that much variety, maybe, but they all have their own characteristics...

Like once when driver Mick West and I came from Wellingborough with the West Drayton empties. I was thrilled by our engine for the day - a shiny ex-works Class 45 Peak. After a long trundle back, we entered the branch at Knighton. Dawn was breaking and, in the cramped second man's side of the loco, I fought hard to stay awake. Until Mick suddenly brought me back to earth with a jolt.

'Right, I've done my bit, Tony. Do you want to take it back across the branch?'

I accepted eagerly. But the vacuum-braked train took some getting used to. Too little and the brake barely bit, too much and you would be almost at a standstill! For a while the wretched thing seemed to have a mind of its own, but after a while I mastered it. The best technique was to brake quite heavily, then take off the brake just as it began to bite. Mick chuckled at me. Blowing out smoke from his cigar he confided that most drivers had trouble learning vacuum braking.

'It's like a stubborn horse, you need to master it before you can control it properly.'

I managed it in the end, but like many others I always felt more at ease with a gauge that read 72.5 p.s.i. rather than 21 inches.

Another event whilst on 'alien' traction was with two Class 25s and another ex Burton driver, Ray Bartram. We'd left Croft on a heavy ballast train bound for Mantle Lane, but the weight of the train combined with Desford Bank became too much for two little type 2s. Half way up they gave up on us. No matter what we did we couldn't move them another inch. Ray stopped the train whilst I went forward for assistance. The area's signal post telephones had failed, so I had a pleasant Sunday afternoon stroll to Bardon Hill box (Bagworth box having closed by then). The guard meanwhile had gone back to Desford to protect the line. So, as I said, it was usually a change to get on the footplate of other locos - but sometimes it wasn't.

Desford was the location for the next story, which took place in the early hours. We'd left the colliery and worked a Didcot Power Station train as far as Landor Street, where we were to be relieved by a Saltley crew. Saltley mess room was always packed with train crews. The majority of them were Saltley men, but there were always crews from other depots awaiting trains for every direction. You'd be lucky to get a seat most days. In that case you'd have to rough it in Landor Street cabin. There you'd constantly be disturbed by other train crews ringing the power box or filling their mash cans. The cabin would just get warm - then another crew would arrive, swinging the door wide open so the cold wind whistled through. Or else, just as a game of crash reached a tense bit, the phone would ring and a Brummie signalman's voice would ask: 'Have you got Barrow Hill men in the cabin as we're just dropping him down.' So it was always better to squeeze into the Saltley mess room if you could. This particular day we were lucky and found a table alongside another Coalville crew awaiting a train of empties from Didcot. Their guard was the efficient but comical Dougie Elliot who was forever playing little tricks on people. The older drivers found it annoying - but to us young lads he was a star attraction. One of his favourite tricks was to hide somewhere and talk into his empty mash can so that it sounded uncannily like the Tannoy that the Saltley TCS used to summon crews to their trains.

'Coalville men for 6M50. Coalville men for 6M50,' he'd cry from behind a partition.

The crew would stand up and gather up their stuff - then someone would notice a grinning face over by the door.

'Sit down again lads - it only Dougie again!'

My driver that day was a young passed man or relief driver who sat filling in his driver's ticket. Once he'd finished eating, the guard went upstairs to see the TOPS clerk to see where our return working was.

'Two back in the plant.'

That meant two or three hours to wait. It could have been worse. I once waited twelve hours in there. Sometimes we'd pass the time with a couple of pints at the Three As, the Olive Branch or the Queens), but on this occasion we just sat reading the paper and chatting.

Eventually we were called out around midnight. Our train was just dropping down to Landor Street. We relieved another Saltley crew, who seemed glad to finish and get off home. Our outward journey had been via the South Leicester, but we were to return via Tamworth. The guard and I shared the second man's seat. Eventually we pulled up on the boards at Coalville, in the hope that someone would take the empties on to Desford where they were required for refilling in the morning. No such luck. Our shift was far from over...

'Desford, lads!' announced the TCI.

'Oh well,' said the driver. 'You can't win 'em all. It shouldn't take us long.'

Twenty minutes later we dropped off the guard at the sidings so he could set the points for an empty road. We would then proceed a train length over the points and ground signal, change ends, and then propel the whole train back into the sidings. It was nearly 2 am and being out in the sticks meant that we changed ends in darkness. A bitterly cold wind blew and cut our faces. As we climbed into the back cab we noticed straight away there were no heaters on.

'Bloody hell,' said the driver. 'Get some heating on in here. It's freezing.'

I felt around the switch panel until I came across the cab heaters and foot warmers. A quicker source of heat was the hotplate. The element could be glowing red in a few minutes so I switched that on too. But I hadn't noticed the rolled-up newspaper that someone had stuffed between the lower window surround and the back of the stove. As we began to set back into Desford Colliery sidings the paper burst into flames. I pushed back in my seat to keep the top of my body away from the flames. In the light of the flames I could see the driver's panicky look.

'What the hell's going on, Tony? Put it out quick!'

I looked around the cab, but there was nothing available. Our traps were in the other end, ready for going on to Coalville holding sidings. In desperation I grabbed an unburned corner of the flaming paper and chucked it out of the window. A quick pain and the smell of burning meant that my hand was minus a few hairs now. But luckily there was no serious damage.

'Phew, that was close,' said Dave. 'Didn't you see that paper behind the stove?'

'No, it's too dark in here.'

I looked back to see if the paper had gone out - but it hadn't. It had fallen into the undergrowth and set the bank alight.

'Oh no.' The driver had already guessed. 'It's set the bank alight, hasn't it? Get the portable fire extinguisher and put it out before it spreads and burns the box down.'

I grabbed the heavy extinguisher, jumped down and hurried towards the scene. Across the fence, in the middle of the field, a number of whitish-grey blobs moved around the field. My heart began to beat faster - until I realised it was just a few sheep who'd been disturbed by a noisy train and some clot carrying something. Reaching the fire, I thumped the plunger (which hurt my hand) and squeezed the grips together. A white cloud gushed out but the flames just flared up. Oh dear, what was it I'd learned at the fire prevention course? Oh yes: point it at the base of the fire. My second blast put it straight out, leaving just a wisp of smoke rising lazily into the night air. After checking for flames and blasting twice more for luck I began to head back towards the sound of our loco in the pit yard. The bobby in the signalbox watched me with a puzzled face. Should I explain what had happened? No, in the early hours of that cold morning I had the devil in me. If he asks I'll tell him, I thought, otherwise I won't.

The dolly clunked off to let our engine out. The two dim marker lights approached slowly and I climbed aboard. On the way back we had a laugh about it.

'What do you think that signalman made of it?'

'Don't know, he never asked.

12: All Change

My trainspotting days seemed numbered! Not many people could work on locos all day and then spend their spare time watching them! Other interests began to surface. A group of girls had begun to hang around Moor Street bridge and slowly began to pick us off one by one. Before long the mating game had claimed us all.

Some of us had been to see Quadrophenia - a film about Mods and rockers and their seaside riots during the Sixties - and we'd adopted the mod lifestyle, dressing smart and going to discos and clubs. At weekends we rode our Lambrettas and Vespas up and down the country, sometimes doing hundreds of miles in a day. We even formed our own club - the Burton Brewers Scooter Club. And it is still around today. My life was just like that of a Sixties mod - but without the riots and drugs! We just went round the scooter rallies, downed a few beers and generally had a good time.

But I had a double life! Some months previously I'd also invested in a better motorbike for getting to work. The gang of greasers who hung about near where I lived were mightily puzzled. I'd arrive home on the noisy motorbike, clad in all my biker's gear - then after tea I'd emerge in my parka and potter off on my scooter!

Still, once you have the railways in your blood it's there to stay. Other interests come and go, but you can never say a final goodbye to the roar of a Class 47 and the whiff of diesel exhaust. Some of Coalville's second men were still railway fans and they regularly talked me into going on one last trip - 'just for old times' sake'.

Our very last trip was a jaunt to York. Getting round depots was no longer a problem now that we had our official ID cards and HV vests and amongst the many different diesel classes on shed stood the impressive A3 pacific Flying Scotsman, in to have her footplate re-boarded. How could I imagine that before long I would be having a cab ride in her at one of the well-known Coalville Open Days?

By now I was courting a girl from Ashby, so my routine was an exhausting one. Burton to Coalville in the morning, then back home, then over to Ashby at teatime to pick her up, then into Burton for a drink, then taking my girlfriend back to Ashby, before finally returning to Burton. Only to repeat the routine the next day and the next. The outcome of all this, apart from wearing out the A50, was that I got totally fed up with the travelling.

One of the drivers who I talked to about it asked why I didn't go for a railway job nearer home. One of his relations was a relief signalman and reckoned that several vacant signalling posts were soon to be advertised. One was at Egginton Junction. After some thought I decided to put in for it.

For the next few weeks though I wrestled with my conscience. Where did I actually belong? In the end, I decided that Coalville was my place and so I cancelled my application. Somehow I'd find a way coping with all the travelling.

A couple of weeks afterwards, while on shed, the TCS came up and told me that someone wanted to see me.

'Who is it?' I asked.

'It's Mr Mackintosh, one of the managers from Derby.'

'Manager from Derby?' I was puzzled. And a bit apprehensive. 'What does a he want to see me for? I haven't done anything wrong.'

'Don't ask me. He's waiting for you in the office.'

After pulling myself together I ambled through our roster clerk's office towards the pay room. Through the glass I could see the manager. Our clerk - Roy Storer - was hard at work in some big ledgers. A proper railway clerk from the old school, Roy would never give you anything more than your due, so they said. But neither would he diddle you. Roy never missed a trick, and he always knew most of what was going on. I decided to ask him, so I could prepare myself for the worst.

'Roy, do you know what he wants me for?'

'It's about your new job, Tony. You've been accepted as a signalman at Egginton Junction.'

'Oh no! Well, thanks for letting me know.'

He looked puzzled at my reaction. I walked to the pay room door and knocked.

'Come in,' bellowed a voice.

I entered the smoke-filled room to see a large man drawing on a smouldering pipe. He wore a dark suit but wasn't so much like the average railway gaffer, more like an ordinary man in the street.

'Take a seat, er, Tony isn't it?'

I acknowledged with a nod.

'Right, Tony. It's about your transfer in grades. You've put in for signalman at Egginton Junction. And I'm pleased to tell you that you've got the job. I'm here to discuss your salary and shift patterns.'

Oh dear! I'd sent a cancellation well over a week ago, but with railway bureaucracy the way it was, the message obviously hadn't got through.

After giving me a job description and a rundown of the pay scales he asked me if I had any questions. So I had to come clean.

'Look, I'm really sorry for wasting your time, Mr Mackintosh, but I've been doing a lot of thinking and I've decided I'd rather stay here.'

Time for the fireworks! Mr Mackintosh drew deeply on his pipe, looked at me over his spectacles. Then he took them off and fixed me with a stare.

'What, you mean you don't want the job?'

'No, not really.'

Slowly and deliberately he screwed up my application form and tossed it into the litterbin. Just as I prepared myself for a right dressing-down his face broke into a smile.

'Well, that's that then.'

'I'm really sorry to mess you about,' I insisted.

'That's alright, Tony, it's got me out of the office. And I've got my expenses. Don't worry about it. But you can mash me a cup of tea before I go back.'

He stood up and reached out to shake my hand. Following me into the mess room he sat and chatted to the other chaps while I mashed a big pot of tea for everyone.

Not that I was under any illusions: if it had been another gaffer, not so friendly, they'd have made me go to Egginton anyway and everything would have been quite different. Mr Mackintosh though was a down-to-earth sort, someone who had come up through the grades, unlike the ones who were just put there because they were supposed to be clever and read up a lot about the railways.

And so I went back to being just an ordinary second man. To hell with the travelling, I thought, I'll do this forever. I was happy to carry on. When it came to it, I felt like I was being paid for enjoying my hobby. So why should I complain?

47286 awaits departure in Swains Park. This location has long gone, but another Swains Park open-cast opened on the upside in 2001. Photo: John Tuffs.

13: A Dog's Life on the Railway!

Railwaymen enjoy a laugh. Like most workers, they often do things they shouldn't but the very nature of railway work stops us getting too playful. What starts off as a simple joke could easily prove fatal and few railwaymen are prepared to go anywhere near that line.

Some of us have been awfully close to that boundary, though, as my next tale shows. No specific rule existed to say that what we did was wrong, and none of us considered it especially dangerous. You may think differently...

It was a fresh and sunny morning. On our way back from Rugeley power station we were braking for the junction at Lichfield Low Level. My driver was the same passed man involved in the bankside fire at Desford. I'd been worrying about a problem I faced the next day. Mum and Dad were stopping at my sister's house for a couple of days and it meant I'd have to leave Geordie, our pet Labrador, home alone. He'd never been on his own before and I wasn't sure how he'd behave.

'Bring him with you then,' said Dave as we passed round the curve to the high level.

'Don't be silly,' I said. 'We can't do that.'

'You can if you want to,' he insisted.

Awaking next morning at 01.45, I looked out of my bedroom window at a world shrouded in freezing fog. I looked longingly at my warm and cosy bed - but I wouldn't be back in it for many hours. Geordie opened one eye, just as he did every morning. He probably wondered what on earth I got up to at such an unearthly hour. Well, today he was going to find out!

After getting washed and changed I fetched Geordie off his chair. He stretched and yawned and looked at me suspiciously. He usually had his walk last thing at night, so he wasn't expecting another one. The icy wind made him even more reluctant, but after a brisk walk around the square he perked up and jumped happily into my old van.

At the depot Geordie stayed in the van while I went to book on. In the office were the TCS, Dave, our guard and a few other chaps.

'Have you brought him?' whispered Dave.

'Yes, he's in the van.'

'No! I was only kidding. You haven't really, have you?'

Then I saw his grin. He was having me on. He didn't really mind, and if he did it was too late now.

Ten minutes later we walked across to the 56 loco that was ticking over on shed road. After stashing my bag, lamp and mash can in the cab I went to fetch Geordie. He sprang out of the back. Once at the loco I had to lift the heavy hairy hound on board.

Certain signalmen in Mantle Lane box would pull off the dolly for the 03.30 Rugeley, knowing it would be going light engine to Overseal. Today was no exception.

'Quick, Tony, look who's coming.'

A quick glance confirmed that Jack Manley, the shed driver, was hurrying across to see what was I up to. He didn't like anything untoward going on and it was in our interest to leave the shed as quickly as possible!

'Phew, that was close,' said Dave, looking back into the foggy gloom at the fading silhouette of a small figure in BR driver's cap holding a shed brush.

We passed through Swannington Crossing and accelerated through Coleorton Cutting towards Overseal. After changing ends over the dolly to go onto our train Geordie and I walked with our guard to examine and brake test the train. The dog was in his element. Rabbits ran for their lives and pheasants flew up from the bank chattering angrily at bring disturbed. Smaller birds fluttered and chirped in the trees. Not to be left out, an owl hooted from somewhere down the Measham and Donisthorpe branch.

Calm returned to the dark and misty sidings as we walked back to our engine. As I heaved the dog back onto the footplate the driver gave a short note on the horn to let the signalman in Moira know that we were ready to leave. The signal arm raised with a clunk and we set off for Rugeley.

I'd been worried about Geordie's reaction whilst on board, as Class 56s can be very noisy and aren't renowned as smooth-riding locos. But I stroked his head and in a few moments he seemed fine. Our journey was uneventful and whilst unloading we ate our sandwiches. I'd brought a tin of dog food and a bowl too. There can't be many dogs that have eaten their dinner in the cab of a diesel loco.

After the usual backing out and run round, we began the journey back to Mantle Lane. After negotiating the curve at Lichfield we accelerated to maximum line speed towards Wichnor Junction. I could see a wicked gleam in Dave's eye

'Here, Tony,' he said, 'can you get Geordie in my seat?'

'What for?'

'We're going to trick old Pipesey at Fine Lane.'

Fine Lane is a manned crossing. One of our guards had broken his arm a short while back and was based there doing light duties.

'Come on, you hold down the second man's hold-over button, then I'll take it while you get him in the seat.'

I tapped on the seat and Geordie obediently jumped into place. We both stooped down in the cab, but Dave was still very much in charge of the train and regulated the power handle accordingly. It looked hilarious as the large dog sat there panting and looking quite unperturbed. As we approached the crossing the stable-like door opened and the large form of Pipesey appeared.

'There he is,' said Dave. Keep down now.'

As we approached Pipesey extended a wave in our direction. Then his friendly grin gave way to a look of horror. His arm dropped, then we were past him.

'Right,' Dave said as we passed, 'let's get back in our places.'

Geordie jumped onto the cab floor and we both got back in our seats. A couple of minutes later we approached Alrewas signal box, which had a direct phone link to Fine Lane. The signalman still had the telephone to his ear as he appeared at the window with a puzzled look. Acknowledging his wave we went on our way, laughing about our joke for the rest of the journey.

That was Geordie's first and last cab ride! He never rode the main line with me again, though he often accompanied me whilst on shed or frost precautions.

After his fracture mended the poor chap at Fine Lane went back as a Coalville guard. Sometime later he took a chargeman's job at Drakelow Power Station, then decided to get a railway job in Scotland. I saw him on his last day. By that time I was a relief driver and had worked the train into Drakelow C-station. We shook hands and wished each other luck.

'Oh, and watch out for dogs driving trains,' I said as I left the room.

He looked at me with astonishment.

'What do you know about that?'

My train would have to wait a little while longer while I told him the whole story.

'I'm glad you told me,' he said. 'I've always wondered if I was seeing things that day. I even doubted my sanity. I rang the Alrewas signalman and told him. He thought I'd been drinking or taking drugs. He was even going to report me!'

14: The Trouble With Jim

As time went by I noticed a pattern to the drivers I worked with. With some I could go weeks without anything untoward happening; with others all sorts seemed to happen. With Jimmy Jackson for instance, another ex-Burton man who'd spent some years at Saltley before arriving at Coalville. Whenever Jim and I were booked on together something seemed bound to happen. Jim was a decent sort, but he had a habit of grumbling at you for the least little thing. Nor was he the only one. Much of it was down to generation gap. You had youths spending all their whole working day with men old enough to be their dads (or even granddads!). But it worked most of the time. These older men had been lads themselves, so they knew what it was like for us.

As far as his outlook on life and the railways Jim was typical of his era. His catchphrase was 'who's fetching the chips?' He always parked his beaten-up Ford on top of the slope of the dock (loading road). When asked why he always parked in the same spot he told us that his battery was on its way out - a condition it must have been in for many years!

One week Jim and I were booked together on the 07.41 Rugeley, which had been diverted on certain days to Drakelow. On a damp and misty Monday morning we left the west end sidings bound for the power station. I was beginning to get itchy feet and I told Jim that I intended to put my name down for jobs at the power station and at the local breweries. One of the gaffers at the power station was Harold Wildgust, driver of the last Tutbury Jinny and a friend of Jim's since their days at Burton loco.

'You want to go and see Harold,' Jim advised me. 'If they're after people he'll get you in.'

As we approached the dip at Tugbys he applied the brakes, but with the wet and greasy rails our loco picked her wheels up and we slid through at almost twice the 20 mph speed limit. The loco rolled from side to side, making us most uncomfortable. After putting down sand, taking the brake off and then reapplying it Jim managed to bring us down to the correct speed.

On reaching Drakelow I went off to find Harold. He took down my details and promised to let me know if anything came up. But it turned out they were actually laying men off, so I never did get a job there.

The next day saw us heading for Rugeley. As usual, we had to wait for a path between Lichfield and Armitage Junction. Four or five expresses were due through before we could go, so to pass the time I scaled the embankment to have a nose around the field at the top. To my surprise it contained some of the biggest mushrooms I'd ever seen. I called down to Jim and our guard, and the three of us were soon filling our sandwich bags with them. After we'd got all we wanted we returned to the engine just as the signalman pulled off.

The following day found us Rugeley-bound again, this time with an extra passenger on board. Coalville shunter Alfie Lichfield had the job of covering Cadley Hill colliery. The regular shunter, Bud Abbot, was off for some reason and the busy pit needed manning. As usual we had to put up with Alfie's moaning.

'Why is it always me?' he grumbled. 'There's plenty of other blokes.'

After we let Alf off at Swadlincote Junction, Jim gave our Class 56 full power. Just as I took a cheese sandwich out of my bag and bit into it there was a loud bang from the engine room.

'What the blazes...?'

We'd only got up to 25 mph when it happened. The power went straight away. Red fault lights came on and the cab was filled by oily black smoke. After opening the windows and doors to get rid of it we came to a stand at DY 126 signal, the one that protects and allows trains into Drakelow.

'It don't look good at all,' said Jim. 'Go and tell Derby it looks like we're a failure. I'll check her out.'

The signalman put the peg back to danger and told me to keep him posted. I got back to the loco to find the engine ticking over in a very sickly manner. The body shook from side to side on its bogies. Jim was a conscientious sort, so I wondered why he hadn't shut it down. I would have done. Then again, it was nothing to do with me. It would be unheard of for a young driver's assistant to tell an old hand what to do.

'I'd better shut it down and take a look,' said Jim.

With that he disappeared into the engine room carrying his Bardic hand lamp and shut the door. I stood and waited, feeling awkward at having nothing to do. A couple of minutes later he emerged.

'I can't see anything. You go in and have a look.'

Delighted to be involved, I took his hand lamp and went into the fume-filled engine room. Immediately my feet felt hot. Shining the beam down I saw they were bathed in hot black oil. In the aisle of the engine compartment large pistons, con rods and other damaged pieces lay everywhere.

'I don't think we'll chance restarting her,' said Jim when I re-entered the cab. I think it was sarcasm. Jim was a bit of a joker sometimes and had a strange sense of humour when things went wrong.

Half an hour later an engine came out of the power station to drag us in. The same one then took our dead 56 back light to Coalville.

'New engine job there,' said the shed man. 'It'll cost them, that's for sure.'

Indeed it did: 56042 was bound for a long spell in Doncaster works.

*

Sometime later they started to run some night 'Rugeleys' again. Jim and I were booked together for a week on one.

'Where's your Bardic lamp?' said Jim as we walked to our engine one night. 'You know you should carry it whilst on duty.'

I had no excuse. It was still in my locker. Looking across at Jim I saw that he didn't have a lamp either - that's why he'd got annoyed with me.

'Where's yours then?' I asked.

'That's not the issue,' he snapped.

We had with us that bitterly cold night a young guard by the name of Nigel Folgate who'd passed out just a few weeks previously.

'I've got my lamp, Jim,' he piped up.

'Excellent, Nigel. You can't get these secondmen motivated to do anything,' he added with a grin that typified his odd sense of humour.

Our journey was uneventful and we backed down into the plant. As one train was already being unloaded we stood down the bottom behind a dolly awaiting our turn. Time for a cuppa! What could be more cheering on such a bitter night when the frost lay so thickly? As soon as the mashing can had boiled I popped in three tea bags and lifted the cab-to-cab phone to tell the guard.

'Just mashed, Nigel.'

'Thanks. I'm on my way.'

A minute later Nigel climbed through the cab door and handed me his mug. As I began pouring the tea there was a loud thump right behind me. I turned to see our guard lying unconscious on the cab floor!

'What the...?'

Jim and I leapt from our seats and frantically tried to bring him round.

'Tony, phone the plant control and tell them what's happened.'

I opened the cab door and slid down the icy handrails. Grabbing the phone I willed them to answer straight away. I tried desperately not to panic.

'Control room...'

'This is the second man of the train standing down the bottom. Our guard's been taken ill. Can you get someone to us straight away.'

'Right,' he said. 'Our first aider's on his way. I'll call an ambulance as well.'

Back at the loco I found Nigel still on the floor. Jim had loosened his collar and was feeling his forehead.

'He's breathing alright. Are they sending someone?'

I told him what the control room operator had said. Having done everything we could think of we sat and waited. It seemed like ages. Then I saw headlights moving towards us in the fog.

'They're coming!'

Moments later two plant workers climbed aboard with a first aid box.

'How long's he been out?' asked one. 'Has he come round at all since it happened?'

We told him all we could. He asked us the guard's name and called it out several times. Nigel's eyelids began to flicker, then he opened them and his eyes rolled in their sockets. His head lolled from side to side, then his eyes opened fully and in the dim light I could see him trying to focus on us one by one.

'Do you ache anywhere?' asked the first aid man. 'Have you banged your head or any other part of your body?'

Nigel shook his head. Rubbing his eyes he sat up and buried his face in his hands.

'What happened?' he asked in a muffled voice. 'I just came in from the back cab to have a cup of tea when... I can't remember. Everything just went black.'

'Seems like you fainted,' said the first aid chap. 'It was getting out of one hot cab, going out in the freezing night, then coming back in this hot cab. We'll take you to the rest room and keep an eye on you for a bit. If you're alright when your train leaves you can go back with your mates.'

'We'd better cancel the ambulance as well,' said the other one.

With that they lifted Nigel back to his feet and helped him down the steps before taking him off in their van. Jim and I glanced at each other and then at the empty mug. After we had finished unloading we ran round our train with the intention of contacting the depot for orders.

'They'll either send another guard out or we'll have to back these into a siding and go back light engine.'

Just then the plant workers' van appeared and dropped off Nigel. He looked much better and was well enough to accompany us back home. I saw to the ground frames and couplings for him. It had been a long night and the three of us were glad to be back at Coalville.

Neither of us could guess at the time, but Jim and I would be involved with illness again. Unfortunately, this time it would be Jim's...

It happened when Jim and I were together once again on a Rugeley job. This time it was daylight and we were accompanied by our usual guard and a younger trainee guard. After unloading about three parts of the train Jim began to complain of stomach pains, which gradually got worse as we got towards the last wagons.

'I'm not going to be able to drive like this,' he told me. 'You're going to have to do it. Come and get in the chair.'

I was happy to drive, but the route could be a problem. Our way back was a relatively new one to us - via the mid Cannock branch to Walsall, run round on the goods line at Ryecroft Junction, then back via Brownhills and Lichfield. Coalville drivers had only just learnt it, and they tended to do the driving themselves until they got to know the route better. There weren't many second men - including me - who knew the route at all.

Just then the cab door opened and the young trainee appeared. Seeing me in the driver's chair he naturally handed me the drivers slip.

'The guard says you can go when you're ready,' he said. 'And he says, can I ride up front to look over the road?'

Jim seemed to be getting worse and his loud groans made the young guard think twice about joining us!

'Look, Jim,' I said, 'you can't go back like that. Let's call help. Anyway, I don't know the road.'

Maddened by pain he stared at me angrily.

'I'm not going to any hospitals around here,' he snapped. 'You'll be alright driving. Just take your time.'

The signal came off one yellow and we set off. I drove as safely as I could. Jim would be of no help to me - by now he was on the floor holding his stomach. (Then he disappeared into the engine room and lay across the second man's seat.) Anything it seemed to try and alleviate the pain. The young guard looked at me for reassurance but I could give very little. Having to get us to Ryecroft in one piece I could have done with a little moral support myself and wished our proper guard could be with us.

We finally made it to the signal before Walsall tunnel, where we had to uncouple and run round. The guard climbed aboard. By now Jim was trying to sleep to escape the pain. Our guard had been oblivious to the situation until then.

'What shall we do?' he asked.

'Wait till we drop in behind the signal to change ends,' I said. 'Then you go on the phone and ask the signalman to call an ambulance.'

Jim must have been catnapping as he suddenly turned round and shouted at us.

'I've told you once, there's no way I'm going into hospital here. I'll go to Burton or not at all.'

So that was that. The young trainee returned to the back cab and I couldn't really blame him. It comforted me to have an older hand guard present. After the run round we headed back across the South Staffs. Jim had managed to change ends with us whilst in the platform but refused any other help. He managed to drop off again and with an air of confidence, I drove the train towards Burton. Jim awoke again at Barton under Needwood.

'Shall we call someone now we're getting close to Burton?' I asked.

'I'm feeling a little better,' he said. 'Thanks all the same. Just you carry on to Coalville now.'

Jim seemed to improve as we made our way up the branch. As usual we were relieved on the boards by another crew. Jim said he'd be alright to drive back to Burton and thanked me for what I had done.

The next day I heard that he'd gone into hospital - to have kidney stones removed!

It was a couple of weeks later before I saw him again, in the mess room at Coalville.

'I was hoping to see you today, Tony. Wait there, I won't be a second.'

He went off and came back a few moments later with a large box of mixed fruit.

'That's for helping me out when I needed it. Thank you.'

15: Working Supper

The railways have never cared much about the social lives of their staff. But at least we could swap shifts if we needed to, a practice that went on at every rail depot. I'd intended to book time off for my 18th birthday, but it slipped my mind and I found myself down for 18.00 ferry work throughout the week of my birthday. And it was too late to do any swaps.

My mate that week was Johnny Clay - or Dave as he was known to his mates. At the start of the week, whilst ferrying engines around the East Midlands, I told him about my forthcoming birthday.

'That's nice, Tony. Are you doing anything special?'

Gloomily I told him that all my lieu days had been used up and as I couldn't swap shifts I'd be spending the week working.

'I'm not that bothered,' I said. ' I can always catch up at the weekend.'

'Not to worry,' said Johnny. 'We'll have ourselves a little birthday tea at work, eh?'

After a little planning we each knew what to bring. When my 18th birthday finally came I arrived at work at 18.00 and found Johnny in the mess room chatting to other chaps.

'Have you brought the stuff, Johnny?'

'Yes, I've got it. But I've got some bad news: we have to take the Jocko to Leicester.'

And so I spent my 18th birthday on an 08 shunter, tickety-bumping at 15 mph all the way to Leicester. On the ancient hot-plate a pork hock was boiling away, as were the trimmings for my birthday tea. A cork was popped and Johnny filled our mugs with his home-made wine. A proper spread in the mess room would have been better, but apart from being splashed with boiling water every time we hit a bad joint it didn't turn out to be a bad birthday after all.

A few weeks later Eddie Brooks and I were on a Didcot job. We called it a 'Didcot' after the train's final destination, but we were only booked to take it as far as Landor Street, just outside Saltley depot. We'd dropped down the branch and stood at a signal at Branston awaiting the road. I went to inform the signalman at Derby power box our train reporting number and destination at signal DY 138.

'Two to go by, mate, and I'll have you on the move,' the power box told me.

As the first rushed train by I shouted to Eddie 'One more, Ed' and then I went off to have a wee down at the side of the loco. With the frosty morning and the hot brake blocks the steam rose into the air. For devilment - and we've all done it - I aimed at another hot block, taking care not to breathe in. Just then the second express dashed through. A moment later the signal came off single yellow. The driver's side window suddenly dropped down.

'Come on,' yelled Eddie. 'He's pulled off.'

A cloud of foul-smelling steam rose up enveloping him. With a muffled curse his head shot back in.

'You dirty bugger!'

I could hardly climb the steps for laughing. Brookie, as he was known, had been the butt of my pranks many times before. It's not nice to give chewing gum to men with false teeth!

In those days I played a lot of pranks on the old boys - but only those I knew I could get away with it. Cyril Kendrick, for instance. One day he would be all strict, grumbling at you throughout the shift; the next time he'd be pulling your leg and having a laugh. This in turn meant we could do the same. But before sharing the more light-hearted times I had with Cyril, I have to tell you of a more sinister thing happened as we took a light engine to Leicester...

After the over bridge at Bagworth the line veers left, leaving a blind spot until it straightens up further on. We were at maximum line speed when all at once we were on top of a gang of platelayers. They scattered in every direction and how we missed them I'll never know. It shook us no end, and for the rest of the journey we felt most uncomfortable about the near loss of life. They should have posted look-out men in both directions to warn of approaching trains. Where theirs was I'll never know, but they certainly had a lucky escape!

Drakelow shunt frame as it was in 1988. The frame controlled movements on and off both east and west arrival and departure roads and the sidings. Photo: Anthony Gregory

16: Footplate Food

For good stories the diesel era can never compete with the steam age. Breakfast prepared on a shovel over the firebox of a steam loco is a hundred times more fun than a fry-up on the hotplate of a diesel. But there were plenty of ex-steam men around and they still had a knack for making a loco cab breakfast especially delicious. Fry-ups were common, especially on a Friday. If you'd been in a happy crew they'd all bring in food and share it. Cheese on toast, soup, sandwiches - we'd have all sorts. An onion wedged next to a Class 47 exhaust manifold was delicious.

Hot drinks - or a 'mashing' as it was often known - were brewed in a mash can or billy can, the same vessels used by the old steam crews. No self-respecting member of a train crew would come to work without one. Some old hands still had their trusty cans from the steam era. These white enamel cans had a carrying handle of thick wire, a side handle to steady it while pouring, and a lid which doubled as a small cup. Later versions were usually made of aluminium. After adding tea, milk and sugar, the can would be whirled round by its handle. This took the place of stirring.

Whilst climbing aboard a loco, some men would put their bag, lamp and can onto the footplate and climb up unimpeded. Others would struggle up with their equipment weighing on their arms and shoulders. The first method was the best, but there were risks. Chaps would often pull their bags into the cab, put their Bardic lamps on the desk but before they could pick up their can - crash! - their mates slammed the door with it in. That happened many times.

One lesson I learned was to be wary when making milky coffee! We'd been standing at a signal at Armitage Junction and got off the loco to watch our guard, Dougie Elliot, winding up a herd of cows in the adjacent field. Cupping his hands to his mouth and mooing deeply, he soon had the herd stampeding around the field. But the cows had the last laugh. We turned to see black smoke billowing from our loco's windows and doors. The milk had boiled over onto the glowing hotplate! The stench was so bad we had to wedge open the doors for the journey home. My blackened and gunged-up can took a good hour to clean.

The two Franks - Wood and Bailey - were Coalville depot's star chefs. If ever there was a smell of cooking you could bet it would be one of them. Both were ex-Burton. Bails was a passed man and a good mate of mine. Mr Wood was an old-hand driver.

One Sunday afternoon Bails and I were on the 14.00 frost precautions. Our job was to run the engines up if the temperature dropped below a certain level. A device would set off a bleeper and that was our cue.

'What you got for your snap?' asked Bails.

'Just cheese sandwiches,' I answered after a quick look into my folded bread bag.

'Right, they'll do for our tea,' he said. He held up a large plastic bag. 'Here's your Sunday lunch...'

Bails went on to cook a lovely Sunday dinner with chops and all the trimmings. Plates, condiments, cutlery - he'd thought of everything. It was better than I was used to at home!

Another time we were on 6V76 loading stone in Cliffe Hill. The train was bound for Hayes & Harlington, but we took it only as far as Wellingborough. Bails had asked me to bring one or two bits in with me, and whilst I loaded the train he prepared our lunch. In the front cab he had bacon, sausage, eggs and black pudding on the go, while in the back cab were tinned tomatoes, beans and mushrooms. It was the nicest mixed grill I'd ever tasted!

Another Sunday morning I was on a ballast train between Cliffe Hill and Ellistown. Our booking-on time was 03.00, so to ease the blow I'd bring in the stuff for a nice fried breakfast. As I booked on bleary-eyed I showed the food - enough for three - to the driver and guard. They both nodded approval. After filling our cans with boiling water we climbed into a railway van which would be taking us to the site.

'Soon be time to get the frying pan out,' one of them said on the way.

My heart sank. It was still in my van.

'Oh no, I've forgotten it!'

'Well, that's goodbye to a nice breakfast then,' they said.

We arrived at the work site and after relieving the other crew we settled down on our Class 20s. But the thought of a long and hungry shift was making us all miserable. By one means or another I had to get that breakfast cooked. I decided to have a scout round. I walked all round Cliffe Hill but all I found was a wall tap that might come in handy if we ran out of water for mashing tea. I was just about to give up when I happened to look over at a line of platelayer's vehicles. One of the bigger lorries had large chrome wheel trims.

Problem solved!

Making sure I wasn't being watched I prised off the nearest one. Apart from being muddy it wasn't in bad condition. I filled it with cold water from the tap and took it back to our engine. The other two gave me some very odd looks as I put the water-filled trim on the hotplate. The boiling water soon killed any germs and after I'd given it a good scrub out - hey presto! - we'd got ourselves a makeshift frying pan.

And so we enjoyed our breakfast after all.

After washing the wheel trim I nipped back to the lorry and tapped it back in place. It was just getting light and I wondered if the lorry driver would notice that he had three muddy trims and one sparkling clean one!

Back on the engine the driver turned to me: 'What do you think the driver of that lorry would say if someone told him we'd fried our breakfast on his wheel trim?'

Though not over-blessed with good points, I've always prided myself on my initiative. I'd used it that morning with the wheel trim and I would get to use it many times in the years to come...

Like the occasion I was on 14.00 frost precautions. Again it was a Sunday. The hot water geyser in the messroom kept going out and as the ignition hadn't worked for years we had to rely on the smokers amongst us to provide a light for it. But neither of us were smokers, so unless we could find a match from somewhere we were facing a dry shift without tea or coffee.

'It's no good, Tony, we'll have to drink water.'

We spent another ten minutes at the ignition before admitting defeat. But I hadn't had time to think properly until then.

'Hang on, I've got it.'

Trotting out to a Class 47 I started her up and turned the hotplate on. Most locos carried a spare paraffin tail-lamp in the cab and this one was no exception. I touched an old driver's slip to the red-hot element and quickly lit the lamp. Shutting the loco down again, I took the lamp back to the mess room, lit the geyser and - hey presto! - hot drinks, a happy driver and an early finish.

Another time Woody, Kev Roberts and I were on a Drakelow job. We'd decided to have hot dogs so each of us had brought a contribution - rolls, hot dogs, onions. After loading the train in Rawdon Colliery I began to prepare the meal, aiming to have it ready by the time we dropped down to the bunker at C station. We soon had tears streaming down our faces - where Woody had got those onions from I'll never know! But they were soon frying nicely in the pan. I opened two tins of hot dogs and sliced the rolls in half. We'd have five and a bit sausages and slice the last one three ways.

We finished off our delicious meal with a nice cup of freshly brewed tea. Then the argument started.

'Hang on...' said Frank. 'We've had five and a bit sausages each, three cobs and onions. Out of the ten cobs there should be one left. But there's two.'

We were all adamant that we'd had our quota. The next half hour was spent trying to solve the mystery but without success. In the end we washed up the utensils and prepared to change ends for the return journey.

But the argument rumbled on. The next day it began again...

'Someone must have missed out yesterday,' Frank insisted. 'Unless there was eleven cobs in the pack by mistake.'

'No, we all had the same: three cobs, two with two sausages in and one with one and a bit. No one had any sausages without a cob.'

And so it carried on. Railwaymen like to make their point and win their corner - especially if they're right.

'I know what happened,' said Frank at last. 'Wait until we get to Drakelow and I'll find out for sure.'

When we reached the bunker we got off the loco and went across to a small bin where the rubbish still remained from the previous day - including our tins.

'The answer is in one of those tins,' said Frank. 'If it's not then we'll never know. Have a look for us Tony.'

The first tin was empty, but the second one contained two cold hot dogs. I must have been in such a hurry to serve up the food that I'd not emptied the tins out properly. To this day I'll don't know who went without their third hot dog. It wasn't me and the other two say they didn't. It remains another of those mysteries of railway life!

My last food story took place one winter's morning. This time it was Frank Bailey. We used to take turns giving each other a lift to work and that week it was Bails' turn. At 04.30 I was sipping a hot coffee when the loud click of the gate latch announced Frank's arrival. As I opened the door our two mischievous kittens Mungo and Midge shot outside into the darkness.

'Do you want a quick coffee before we leave?' I asked.

'Yes, can do, said Frank, dropping down his bag and stepping inside.

After our drink I went to fetch the kittens back in. In the grey light of dawn I was dimly aware of pieces of bread all over the yard. A horrified Frank came up close behind me.

'What the... They've scoffed my snap! There's best beef in there.'

I couldn't stop myself laughing. 'There was best beef in those.' I mimicked.

Most of the meat had gone and a sullen Frank picked up a piece of soggy bread.

'I wouldn't have minded if they'd eaten the bread as well. What a waste.'

That only made me laugh even more. But Frank cheered up when I offered to share my grub with him and to make sure he had enough he bought three bags of crisps from the newsagents.

17: The Two Franks

The two Franks featured many times in the stories about my Coalville days. But three tales about the antics of Frank Wood spring to mind...

One day, whilst awaiting a set of empties for loading at Bagworth, he suddenly opted out of a game of crash to ask me a question.

'Tony, can you cut hair?'

'Why?'

'My missus keeps nagging me about the length of my hair. Have you got time to give us a quick trim while we're waiting?'

I couldn't believe what he was asking me.

'Why me? I've never cut anyone's hair in my life. What's wrong with the barbers?'

'I'm not paying their prices. Go on, be a sport.'

To keep the peace I agreed to give it a go. Frank produced a pair of beaten-up scissors. Amid the chuckles of other second men I made a start, first cutting the longest bit at the back, then a bit near the ear. Soon I was quite carried away, snip-snip-snipping away here there and everywhere.

I'd heard a tale about Harry Johnson, the well-known steam driver who finally retired from the railway at 72 after stints as a guard and a cabin cleaner. He had made extra money by cutting hair as he travelled around the railway system. One day, on his way to Wellingborough, he'd drawn up to the junction signal at Knighton to wait for a London bound express to pass.

'Hey up, Harry,' one of the Knighton shunters shouted up at him. 'Any chance of a short back and sides?'

Harry told his fireman to keep an eye on the signal and climbed down with his clippers. He was halfway through the cut when his fireman shouted to him

'He's pulled off Harry.'

With that Harry gathered up his equipment and hurried back to his loco, leaving a somewhat irritated shunter.

'Oi!' he yelled.

'I'll do the other half tomorrow,' promised Harry, and with that they charged off in a cloud of smoke and steam.

Back at Coalville I was thinking that I ought to be charging Frank for his haircut. Stingy blighter! Then I took a step back to admire my handiwork. What a mess! He'd kill me when he saw it! I was just about to confess all and risk his wrath when I was saved by a shout:

'Yours is next on the up Frank.'

'Hurry up, Tony,' urged Frank. 'It don't matter what it looks like, so long as it's shorter. There's only two week's difference between a good haircut and a bad one. I've saved a couple of quid now, that's the main thing.'

And so, amid tittering from various parts of the lobby, we grabbed our traps and made for our train.

A few weeks later I was second-manning Frank on the 06.00 shed. It was a Thursday and the mood in the mess room was good - mostly because at 12 o'clock Roy Storer would be paying out our wages. Mischief was in the air and a bunch of younger second men, myself included, began to tease the older drivers. Frank loved a laugh but sometimes he went a bit too far. This time he appeared at the door with a bucket of water. As soon as we saw him we scarpered. We'd just got around the partition to the kitchen when he let fly.

Splash!!

Water went everywhere and so did railwaymen. With things getting out of hand we decided to calm down a bit. Mops were fetched and Operation Dry Floor commenced. After ten minutes of non-stop mopping and wringing the floor was clean and drying nicely.

'Isn't it funny?' Frank remarked. 'I only threw one bucket of water, yet we've emptied six buckets full down the sink!'

The last of the Frank tales took place in the then newly-opened opencast between Lount and Tonge - aptly named Lounge. The metal coal bunker was still being erected so we were being pad loaded by means of a large-bucketed digger standing on the dock. We'd move several wagons at a time, the pace being controlled by means of two-way radio instructions between the digger driver and us. Most of the drivers were alright, but this one was very uncouth and his language turned the air blue. He hadn't a clue how to communicate properly.

'Right then, driver, move forward. Go on then, keep going, bloody keep going. Right then, stop, woah, bloody stop!'

That's how he was - though most of his adjectives were worse than bloody. It was impossible to do right by him. You were too slow or wouldn't stop in the right place. He didn't have the brains to realise that a heavy coal train couldn't stop just like that. If he'd said 'get ready to stop' there wouldn't have been a problem. But he never did. And, for some reason, it was always those last few wagons that seemed to annoy him most.
'I'll fix this clown,' said Frank. 'He won't have reason to shout tomorrow.'

The next day, as we backed in, Frank produced a square piece of wood with a point at one end. After we had positioned the last few wagons Frank got down and knocked the stake into a pile of coal adjacent to the front of our engine. He'd now be able to use it as an exact marker.

'Wait till tomorrow,' he said with a wink.

The next day Mr Mouth was being his usual nasty self. When it was time for the last move Frank opened our engine right up and we shot forward. The two-way radio crackled with annoyance as the driver came on.

'Steady on, driver. Bloody go steady there!'

But Frank took no notice and didn't slow down until we came up to the stake. Hitting the brakes he stopped the loco exactly beside the marker. The voice that came back to us was full of grudging respect.

'Spot on, driver. Yeah, that'll do yer.'

'There you are,' Frank said to me. 'It doesn't take much to outwit people like that. It should keep him calm from now on.'

The next day the driver came over the two-way radio with a much friendlier tone. Frank did his thing again, but as we approached the marker the driver started yelling again.

'Hey, steady on, slow down. Bloody hell, you'll have to set back now.'

Frank was baffled.

'What's up with him now? We're nowhere near the marker.'

We found out later that we'd been sabotaged. Some of the lads in the cabin had heard about Frank's trick and moved his marker a few feet further down!

18: Our Dated Railway

Night trips to the power station were still second-manned. These were long trains of 'conventionals' - the old 24-ton wagons. I still recall the throaty hiss as the driver operated the temperamental vacuum brakes, taking care not to knock the guard about in his lonely van way down at the back of the train. After entering A/B sidings we would shackle off to save the guard a long walk. He would slip his brake and while waiting for us to come round to him he would pin down the wagon brakes. Giving one of its unmistakable whistles our class 20 would then attach to the brake van and shunt into the empty side to pick up a train of empties bound for Overseal. After the guard had uncoupled his van with a shunting pole we would flyshunt it down an empty road in order to put our empties on to it.

All these procedures were guided with Bardic lamp signalling. The shunter would relay the guard's signals to us.

White up and down = Forward

White light across the body = Come Towards

Green light across the body = Not Far Off, Slow Right Down

Red = Stop.

Red light up and down = Create Vacuum Or Air Pressure

With the last wagon now buffered up to the brake van the guard nipped underneath, coupled the instanter coupling and vacuum pipe. Once 21" of vacuum had been created the guard would pull down the lever in his van, letting in the air and destroying the vacuum in the pipe. This was a brake continuity test, just in case the guard had to stop the train in an emergency. Once tested, the driver would recreate the vacuum and ensure that the brakes were fully off. Once the signal had cleared, a green light would be given by the chargeman and we'd be on our way to Overseal. The last job was mine. As we departed Drakelow by a right-hand curve I would watch for a green from the brake which meant that the guard was aboard and all was well.

Once in Overseal our whole train would have to run down the Measham & Donisthorpe branch so as to back into one of the sidings roads. The second man's job was to relay signals from guard to driver. Many's the night I've scaled the rusty ladder of the old lighting gantry, our regular signal relay point, often in freezing temperatures and heavy rain. My slippery hands would be holding desperately onto both rungs and bardic lamp, looking northwards and awaiting a red light from the guard. Once seen I'd have to hang there by one arm as I adjusted my lamp to red, cursing as the cold rain dribbled down my face and the gantry shook scarily from side to side in the wind. Then came the signal. A white light up and down meant he'd chopped off the brake. Now he had to carry on down the branch to clear the points. Hanging on for dear life by the crook of my arm, I'd change my lamp to white. As I signal up and down as best I can a solitary crow somewhere down that dark branch acknowledges that the driver

56051 Leaves Overseal Sidings in 1979. Photo: John Tuffs.

sees and understands my signal. Once over the points it's red again, then call him back, white across the body. How we managed all those manoeuvres I'll never know!

Another crow call and the train begins to set back slowly. Wagon after wagon squeals, buffers clang together until the last wagon is clear. A red aspect from the guard ends the movement. Gratefully I climb down the ladder and rejoin the driver in the warm cab. The guard pins down the wagon brakes and detaches us from the train. We proceed towards the brake van, re-couple and propel it towards the departure signal. Once off, it's engine and brake to Coalville via a dolly on the down line.

Workings such as this had been practised all over the country for years. At that time, though, the twilight of the conventionals was fast approaching, owing to the increasing numbers of MGR sets coming into service. Merry-go-round trains were faster and easier to unload. Turnarounds were quick, as long as they had a proper MGR circuit. At that time the only two in the area I knew of were Drakelow's A/B station and Ratcliffe. The rest were still time-consuming run rounds.

The days leading up to Christmas were always fun, especially for us younger ones. Christmas Eve 1981 sticks in my mind as a good day. Yet again someone had played the old telephone trick on our TCS. He had five telephones on his desk now and some wag had swapped all the handsets around, so when he'd answer a phone it just kept ringing. Slamming it down he'd pick the next one up, slam that one down - and so on until he got the right one. But you can only play the same joke so many times and today was once too often. Getting his hair off the TCS threw the phone right across the room!

I was looking forward to one of our discos at the Leander Rowing Club that evening. But first I had to book on for one of the many additional ferries taking and stabling locos at Burton loco. My booking-on time was 13.00, so whilst approaching Coalville I passed my booked mate, ex-Burton driver Gordon Sanders. He gestured with his finger, as if to say 'turn around, go back'. He'd probably arranged for us to take an engine off the loco and fetch a last rake of engines down.

I finally arrived at the loco to find it was full of engines but deserted of people. Very odd! As Gordon lived just round the corner in Anglesey Road I decided to nip round to his house.

'What's happening, Gord?' I asked when he answered the door.

'We're not required, Tony. They're all on the loco shut down. The last ones went down at 12 o'clock.'

With that we wished each other festive greetings and I went home to get myself ready for that night's disco.

19: Bobbies, Railway Crime and A Close Call

Police are a necessary force, as most people will agree. As long as they act fairly that is. Like most people I've had a love/hate relationship with them: you're glad they're there when you need them, but when it comes to a ticket or a caution they're not so high on your Christmas card list!

One afternoon whilst driving through Coalville on my way to work I was pulled over by two nasty looking policemen. After twenty minutes of having my car checked and double-checked and being made to feel guilty over nothing they sent me on my way, but not before instructing me to take my documents into Burton police station within seven days. They'd obviously had a bad day and looking for someone to take it out on.

It made me late for work and I got a blast of sarcasm from the TCS. A gang of grinning railwaymen watched as I retold my story. Aware that I was, for once, the centre of attention I decided to give them a story worth listening to! I wasn't the sort to get angry very often, but it was a chance to get it all off my chest...

'Well, these two big bloody coppers pulled me over...' I began

The air turned blue as I voiced my opinions of the police force. Then suddenly the laughter seemed to dry up. A few carried on, but the others looked more serious. I was aware that someone had come in through the door behind me - probably another of the blokes wanting to hear my story. Or so I thought. Still voicing my disgust with the police I turned around to see. I went bright red. Standing right behind me were two more policemen. My mumbled apologies were drowned by a chorus of laughter. As I left the office I noticed that even the two policemen were grinning. As it happened they'd only come to warn us about security. A bomb threat had been received and they wanted us all to be on the lookout for anything suspicious.

This humorous police tale took me back to an incident in my trainspotting years, when every Sunday afternoon we would take a stroll around Burton loco to see what was on. A week previously the only Class 46 'namer' 46026 Leicestershire And Derbyshire Yeomanry had been on shed and had its headcode indicator box smashed in by vandals. We were unaware of this at the time and - like other spotters before us - bumped headlong into two railway policemen. After taking our names and addresses they took us home to speak to our parents. Two weeks later we were summoned to appear before the chief inspector of BT Police at Derby.

My mates, Andy Clarke and Rob Woodman, stood either side of me whilst the inspector tore a strip off us. Then he showed us a very gory film featuring the mutilated bodies of trespassers killed on the railway. It was intended to scare us off the railways for good. After that he calmed down a little.

'Right lads, I think we all understand each other. Any questions?'

'We were all hoping to join the railways when we leave school,' one of us piped up. 'Do you think this will affect our chances in any way?'

'It certainly will!' the inspector exploded. 'None of you will ever work for British Rail now, so you can forget about that here and now.'

With that we all hung our heads and walked out. Five minutes later we were sneaking around Derby loco works to see what was on! Ironically, all three of us made it onto the job and are all drivers.

Children have always been a problem on the railways, especially during the summer holidays. Most train crews have witnessed some hare-brained prank or another. The most horrific was a gang of kids on a bridge hanging a brick down on the end of a rope. Amazingly they were smarter than they looked and pulled up the brick at the last minute. It didn't do the driver's nerves any good, but at least it stopped them being up on a murder charge!

In my time I've driven into a huge stone ball off a church wall and witnessed a shower of bottles come off a bridge over a cutting at Braunston. They sparkled in the air like raindrops in the evening sun then - crash! smash! - they exploded into our cab. Later on I was to have the side drop window of my Class 47 cab put in so violently that I was cut in several places and suffered such deep shock that I had to have several sessions of counselling at Crewe.

But I won't condemn all kids. Some do still stand on fences and bridges and wave innocently to the passing trains.

Old hand driver Ray Frearson and guard Kevin Roberts were working a train from Landor Street via the South Leicester. Both had endured a long shift and entering the branch at Knighton for the last leg of the journey must have been welcome. Ray began to brake for the 15 mph restriction at Saffron lane when suddenly all hell broke loose as they became violently derailed. Their loco, 56070, came to rest next to the parapet of the Saffron Lane road bridge. If it had carried on any further it could have demolished a black wooden cabin which, according to some Leicester men, could have put out half the TV sets in Leicester, being as it was some sort of control room. The cause of the derailment was kids jamming some obstacle in the points.

Due to Ray's derailment all trains heading south to Wellingborough and beyond had to go via Stenson and Leicester. For two nights we had to make that long trudge whilst working the West Drayton. This was the first time I had qualified for mileage payments.

As in any job you have the careful people, the opportunists and the hotheads. Hotheads do things for different reasons. They may be naturally brave; they may not have the imagination to foresee the consequences of their actions; or they may simply do things just to impress others. Whatever the reasons, it's not always comfortable to be with a hothead.

One summer evening I arrived at work for the 18.00 ferry. I parked up and was just about to take the keys from the ignition when someone banged on the window.

'Come on, Tony. Are you ready? We've got to take a 47 to Wellingborough for the return of the Hayes empties. If we shoot off now we'll be back by nine and see the lads in the Snibby for a pint.'

Thinking of the distance between Coalville and Wellingborough I thought it was somewhat unlikely we'd make it. But still, we were conditioned not to question a driver's judgement and so I got my lamp and billy can from my locker and joined him in the office.

'Light engine for Wellingborough, please Bobby,' he said, putting the phone down. 'Come on, Tony, let's get cracking.'

Oh no, I thought, something tells me I'm not going to enjoy this!

Before I start my tale proper I must say that apart from being a bit on the crazy side this driver was a good mate and popular with all the men at the depot. He is also, alas, no longer with us and I am the only remaining witness to the events of that warm summer evening...

We shot off the shed at breakneck speed and came to a stand behind the dolly. Through the open windows we heard the clunk of it coming off and we were on our way. As we passed Mantle Lane box and the site of the old 17C steam shed the crossing gates dropped and the semaphore sprang into the air. Whack! Straight open went the power handle. The engine roared and black exhaust fumes billowed into the air. My fingers gripped the armrests for dear life as we reached speeds of nearly 75 mph. Whenever a well-known bad spot was reached my heartbeat increased and my stomach tightened. Then, as we rode through it, came a sense of relief. The one I dreaded most was at Kirby Muxloe, on the crossing near the golf course. Even at 45 mph we always got a good kick - but at this speed it was anyone's guess. As we approached I closed my eyes and waited, thinking about who would inherit my belongings when I'd gone. Then, after a bit of rocking, we were past it and a flicker of hope returned. The worst part was over: chances are that I might survive the trip after all.

With the back 'un on for Knighton he began to slow down. As we negotiated the bend outside Saffron Lane stadium, up went the signal arm and off we went again. A light engine 47 doesn't take long to reach a high speed and by the time we approached Wigston North Junction we were up to 90 mph - 20 mph over the speed limit! The engine negotiated the sharp left bend and began to waddle like a duck. I think my soul must have left my body in order to watch over events from a safe distance! Suddenly two loud bangs sounded on the left-hand side of the engine. The left-hand wheels must have left the rails! But I was almost past caring by this time. All I knew is that they'd have to break my fingers to loosen my grip on the seat...

Seconds later we were out of it and back on the straight. I turned to see the driver dabbing his brow with his hankie.

'Flippin' heck,' said the driver. 'That was a close call.'

I couldn't speak. I just stared ahead.

'Oh well,' said the driver. 'Let's get back to the matter in hand.'

Back on the straight, we were soon reaching speeds of up to 100 mph for the rest of our journey to Wellingborough. I don't know how, but we delivered the engine safely onto the depot, screwed down the parking brake and climbed down onto solid ground.

'Come on Tony, we've only got ten minutes before our train gets in.'

It's a good walk from Wellingborough depot to the station and my legs wouldn't function properly - probably due to them being turned to jelly! Goodness knows how, but we made our train, running across the boards as it rolled into the station. After an uneventful trip by train and taxi we made it into the Snibston Inn at just about the time he'd predicted. The place was full of railwaymen and after my first pint I began to relax.

'Tony, tell them all what happened.'

I jabbered out my story to the assembled railwaymen. Their reactions were mixed.

'It's a wonder you didn't shift the track.'

'Don't you know your speed limits?'

The rest of the week was no less hair-raising. It seemed to me that some people just never learned from their experiences.

20: Trapped In A '20'

After my alarming experiences on the 18.00 ferry, and the near demise of a Coalville crew, life at Mantle Lane slipped back to its usual pace. That's it for a bit, I thought, nothing else can go wrong surely?

On a glorious summer evening I went to prepare the Class 20s for the night Toton tripper. After my earlier scare with the parking brake the first thing I did with shut-down 20s was to put in the battery isolating switches and start them up before even thinking about the parking brake.

All manner of exterior checks had to be carried out too. As well as the lights, buffers, pipes and fuel gauges I had to look out for cracks in the brake blocks - none of which should be over one inch. The water level in the header tank also had to be checked. For this you had to climb onto the side framing and open the nose-end side door with a T-key. Once in, you had to switch on the light or aim your Bardic lamp at the water gauge at the top of the rear wall. It was always best to leave one of your legs sticking out so that the heavy door wouldn't shut on you. Tonight though the water gauge was obscured by grease and so I had to pull in my leg and reach up to clean it with a cloth.

Slam!

The door always tended to close, due to the slight lean of locos while on shed side. I wasn't that bothered. After satisfying myself that the water tank was full enough, I turned back to open the door. The handle wouldn't budge. I tried it downwards, then upwards, but it still wouldn't budge. Neither would the other door open. I was stuck fast!

But I knew my mate was out in the yard doing a job. All I had to do was bang on the doors. I was panicking a bit now, in case I was in for a noisy and claustrophobic trip to Toton. Bang bang bang, I went. 'Hell-ooo! Let me out!'
Several minutes were spent with these frantic pleas - until a metallic scrape outside the door signalled the arrival of help. My mate had been heading back to the cabin when he'd heard my furious banging.

'You daft bugger - what you doing in here?'

As we climbed down off the loco I explained what had happened.

'You're bloody lucky I heard you,' he said. 'Look over there.'

Indeed, I was lucky. The Class 20's crew were already walking across the yard to start up the locos and head off!

A few weeks later, while on annual leave, I was taking Geordie on his usual morning walk along the railway towards Swadlincote Junction. As we passed by the Stapenhill F.C. ground and walked along the top of the embankment a man approached from the opposite direction trailing a Jack Russell. We nodded to each other, but as we went to pass his dog took one look at Geordie and fled in terror down towards the tracks. Just at that moment a Class 47 passed DY 126 signal down in the cutting. Driven by the late Mick West it was trundling slowly towards Drakelow east at about 10-15 mph. The dog headed straight along the track towards the train. Inevitably the engine went over him. The dog was now so hysterical it didn't even attempt to run out. It just spun round and round on the spot. Unable to look, the dog's owner covered his eyes and tensed up for the final death yelp.

But he was not to hear it that day.

One by one, thirty five fully loaded HAA coal wagons passed over the dog and as the last one clattered clear that lucky little Jack Russell was still there spinning on the spot. The owner and I rushed down. As he picked up the trembling dog I apologised, feeling that it was my place, even though Geordie hadn't so much as looked at the Jack Russell. The owner was too relieved to care.

'It's alright mate, it wasn't your fault. I just can't believe that's happened, can you? I reckoned I'd be going home with just the lead!'

There are two more short anecdotes about the branch. Both sound far-fetched, but they did happen and I believe they deserve recounting...

The first event, which took place at the end of a long hot summers day in 1974, is also recounted in John Smalley's second book Nottinghamshire Railway Ghosts. Day in day out during the long school holidays a group of us cycled down to Moor Street Bridge to spend the day spotting. This particular day one of the lads had a puncture, so we'd had to walk down. As dusk approached we were all ready for home - but not until we had seen the 20.30 southbound mail train. It was often hauled by a Stratford-based 47 and painted up with silver roof and red buffer beam. When it had vanished into the distance, beyond the loco depot, we set off for home.

'Let's nip down Anglesey Road and then walk back along the lines,' one of us suggested.

We all agreed, so at Branston Road we scrambled up onto the bridge and started to walk along the lines towards Stapenhill. The night sky was darker now as we approached the viaduct over the River Trent. Two of us were in front, while myself and the other two followed some yards behind. Both groups were chatting happily about the day's loco sightings when all of a sudden the front two came to a dead stop.

'What yer bloody stopped for!' we cursed as we cannoned into the back of the first two.

They didn't reply, but just stood staring in front of them, towards the middle of the viaduct just beyond the wartime pillboxes.

'What's up?' we asked, frightened by their silence.

We were all looking that way now and as my eyes focused in the poor light I saw what looked like a figure in an illuminated mist. It was possible to make out the head and shoulders, and a long body. But there was something wrong with the legs. They only went as far as the knees – below them nothing was visible. The thing - what else could I call it? - moved slowly towards us. For a couple of seconds we were transfixed – then we pelted as fast as we could, stumbling blindly, scattering the ballast, consumed by terror until we reached Branston road bridge and saw the street lights and the window of a small shop.

We just stood there shivering. We were in shock. One of us was even sobbing openly. It affected him so much that he stopped coming out with us after that.

In the following days we told our story and asked questions about what or who it might have been out there. From the bits and pieces we were able to put together it seemed that, over the years, there had been several deaths on or around that viaduct. Several workmen had lost their lives in accidents during its construction. One hot day many years back, a young fireman from Burton had been drowned whilst swimming in the river with some of his colleagues. Several suicides had been recorded there too, including my father's best friend. And in the early Sixties a crowd of people – including my mother and me in my pram – had watched the river being dragged for the body of a young boy. He'd been playing on the parapet when a passing train had caused him to fall to his death. He was eventually found down the river at Clay Mills.

So just what was it we saw that night?

Exactly a year later a crowd of over seventy people – our schoolmates and their relatives - gathered at the spot, hoping for an anniversary repeat. Nothing appeared. But the viaduct exerted such a strong feeling of dread that a religious man was eventually called in to exorcise the place.

Eight years later, by then working on the railway, I was witness to another strange event. I'd booked on as shed second man at 22.00. The night ferry had returned early and while awaiting the last engine to come on shed, I tended to my duties - setting the road for the last engine, locking up all the locos, bringing in the fog signals/detonators and fixing the large rail blocks in place. This last had been a necessary precaution since some local kids went joyriding on some engines in 1978. Once my duties were completed and the last loco was safely in, the depot would close down for the weekend and the key would be left under the dustbin until 23.59 on Sunday night.

Quite often there would be two or three of us from Burton, and we would proceed home in a leisurely convoy, looking out for each other in case of car trouble. Tonight though, as I set off down the A50 at 02.45 on that dark and drizzly Saturday morning, I was on my own...

At that time the road was being widened and for months there'd been widespread delays as the road workers had moved from one section onto the next. That night the work was near the top of the Alton Hills, right outside Alton Grange where the famous railway engineer George Stephenson had once lived. Drawing up at the temporary lights – on red of course – I allowed myself a wry smile. Not so long ago chargeman/shunter Jack Johnson had been pulling me leg about the place. 'You want to be careful on that A50 at night,' he told me. 'Specially up on the Altons. They reckon on certain nights you'll see George Stephenson in his gig, being pulled along by his favourite horse, Bobby.'

Jack's warning had been greeted by chuckles. Now here I was, on that very same stretch of road. The rain spattered against my windscreen and the radio was on, playing a quiet song through the static crackle. I'd been thinking of ignoring the red light anyway. There was virtually no other traffic around at that time of night and you could see well ahead if anything was likely to come.

Just then, somewhere in the distance behind my van, I distinctly heard the clump of heavy footsteps. Before each footfall came a distinct tap, as if the boots had segs on. Feeling distinctly uneasy now, I listened to the regular metallic chink as whoever it was got closer and closer. The hairs on the back of my neck prickled. Just as the footsteps got close to the back of the van the lights changed and I screeched away.

I was really spooked. The sound was definitely that of someone walking, but there'd been no one in front of me as I'd approached the lights. Tall thick hedges lined both sides of the road, so it was highly unlikely that anyone could have joined the road from the side. The hairs didn't start to go down until I passed the Packington crossroads. Could it have been George Stephenson taking a walk around his estate? Or some tramp making his way down to Ashby? Or was it just the over-tired imagination of a young railway worker eager to get home to his bed? It's a mystery to which I'll never know the answer - and perhaps it's better that I don't!

21: All Out Lads!

The ASLEF strike of 1982 which began on Monday July 5th had its origins in an earlier NUR dispute over the introduction of flexible rostering. After two days the NUR strike began to collapse and many branches returned to work. It was a humiliating situation and after several emergency meetings it was decided that ASLEF, the staunchly militant driver's union, would become involved. Our General Secretary was Ray Buckton, a typical locoman of the old school. On one occasion, during the short dispute, Ray was attacked by an angry commuter on the London underground. But as we were threatened with dismissal the ensuing strike lasted only two weeks. On our return we would be reinstated in groups and each man would lose his seniority. That was fine by me but not for long-serving drivers who were expecting a golden handshake and a railway pension. At Coalville we were 100% behind the action, with the backing of drivers in the NUR. But not all depots fared so well: we heard of drivers leaving depots and flashing their wage packets at the pickets. When the strike ended plans were presented to single-man the bulk of main line work. History was repeating itself. The strike of 1955 also lasted two weeks and ended with a pay rise for the drivers - but the firemen received nothing. Though the 1982 strike wasn't about pay, again it was the second men who would bear the brunt of managerial revenge. They would book on for turns and receive no work. The only job still double-manned was the odd mainline turn, shed, ferry, and the Bardon shunt. Luckily no one suffered in the long run and although it was a frustrating time we would all eventually be absorbed into the system. The line of promotion meant that we were all drivers in waiting. It was ironic that two weeks later the head of the BR board, Clifford Rose, passed away. It left a nasty taste in our mouths.

The months after the strike were bleak ones for us. Rumours of redundancies were everywhere and small groups of second men walked around the town and the yards gloomily pondering the big question. Salvation came in the shape of specials to run coal to top up at the power stations after the dispute - and specials required a second man.

In 1984 four of us received letters informing us that we were to attend the MP12 (driver training) course. To say we were over the moon would be an understatement. The letter also said that all books – i.e. rule book, sectional and general appendix, working manual, electrified lines, traction manuals and a host of others would be required. My plastic carrier bag just couldn't cope under all that weight and I had to invest in something sturdier.

On the morning of 5th March 1984 we met in Room 36 at Wyvern House, platform 1 at Derby. Our instructor was again Bernard Willis, along with several others who would take various aspects of the course in the coming weeks. I wouldn't be seeing Coalville depot for six months, so along with our free passes to Derby I would be saving a fair bit of money.

Alongside us four Coalville men were five from Leicester and five from Derby. We were eased gently into the course, but as each day went by our heads were becoming chock-a-bloc with rules and regulations. Most of us revised at home or on the train, though none would admit to it. Men who'd already done the MP12 course warned us that unless we were prepared to revise we'd simply fail and have to do it all over again. And so, as we went deeper and deeper into the rule books, the enthusiasm we'd had at the beginning started to wane a little. As the days went by we got more fed up and confused, so much so that we would end up daydreaming or doodling on our pads to stem the boredom. And yet we knew we would have to know it all to stand any chance of getting through the 3-day examination in front of the loco inspector.

The Derby lads were by far the cleverest of the bunch, or at least they were seen swotting up the hardest. They were affectionately known as the A-Team, while the four of us Coalville lads had counter-named ourselves the Z-Team. At break times, while Derby lads were busily revising and taking notes, we would nip off for some liquid refreshment or play Nuclear War games with Craig's cigarette papers rolled around a pencil and marked either USAF or USSR. The object was to take each other's bases out.

'You've got no hope of passing this course,' the Derby lads would say, shaking their heads at our antics.

But we had to let off steam somehow and it was only a bit of light-hearted fun. The pressure was tremendous and I heard that two or three courses before ours one bloke had committed suicide over the pressure. One lunchtime Bernard came in and caught us in the middle of another game.

'Tony – what are you doing?'

To his bemusement I explained that I'd just taken out all of my rivals bases in the south.

Towards the end of each week we would dine out at the Alexander. It was pleasant to have a meal with our shandies, but once back in the classroom with a full belly and the sun shining warmly through the windows it was increasingly hard even to stay awake, let alone take in any learning. That summer of 1984 was a hot one, and if some unfortunate person did nod off the instructor would pause and wait for one of us to slap the culprit.

'Thank you for joining us,' the instructor would say as the bloke woke and looked around in embarrassment. 'Is it alright if we carry on?'

At the end of the day though, even with all these incidents, we worked very hard and the instructors knew it. On the wall of the classroom hung a large working model of a loco fuel pump. One part of it was called the helix and this wooden piece, the size of a baked bean tin, found its way into a different bag every night and must have visited the homes of everyone who was on the course more than once. So every night we would all look up to the fuel pump, see that the helix was missing and then search our bags for the offending piece.

We were glad to complete our Rules & Regulations – it had been a headache from start to finish. Little did we know that the Engine would be just as bad. The basic traction in our area was the Class 47 (or four and a half in railway terminology). The basic stuff was fine, until you started going deeply into the air-braking, fuel, water and oil systems. The electrics side of it was even worse, with parallels, series parallels, main and auxiliary generators, traction motors, exhausters and compressors. We went through the lot.

Sometime during all this was 2-week Basic Electrics course – this one even worse than the previous two. It's nice to know that BR liked to train its drivers efficiently, but to me it seemed like a bit too far. We were meant to be train drivers, not electricians! The first day we managed to grasp it, and we even kept up for half of the second day, but as they went deeper and deeper into the subject they just lost us. Even the instructors admitted it was hard going – so what chance had we got? We just sat there and let them ramble on. I'd be sitting there thinking about what jobs I had to do on my motor scooter when I got home, or where I would be going out to that night.

The one fun aspect of the Basic Electrics course was a circuit board made up by some bright spark to demonstrate the functions of fuses, lights, switches and contact breakers. We were encouraged to tamper with this board and one break time I managed to blow the thing up. I don't know what I did, but there was a shower of sparks, a bang and a puff of smoke.

Anyhow, we managed to struggle through the fortnight and then began our revision period for everything we had covered. Anything we still didn't know, now was the time to ask. The inspector who was to pass us out was keen on the Engine - so back we went through it all again. Recite the firing order of the 47? I once woke up from sleep in the early hours doing just that. The 4-stroke cycle - induction, compression, power and exhaust.

We certainly earned our wages from then on…

22: MP12 – BR's Driver Training Course

A few days on the Basic Traction course were spent visiting various places to look around a Class 47. Getting out of the classroom for a few hours really helped renew our enthusiasm. On one of these days we went to Stoke-on-Trent to have a look at a 47 that was sitting in the old bay. The instructor was so pleased by our recognition skills that he let us finish the day at lunchtime - a bonus we had to celebrate with a quick pint!

Next came the fun part - the running out. Split into pairs, we were given our own instructors. I counted myself lucky: the instructor, Steve Holmes, and my fellow trainee were both decent. Steve started us off with a pep talk.

'Right, lads, we'll work this out between us so as to suit everyone. But I want commitment.'

Opting for days, we next met up in the old 4-Shed messroom. Our first train was the 'Jolly Fisherman' holiday special, which ran to Skegness during the summer months. Consisting of about eight coaches hauled by two Class 20s, it started from Burton, ran round at Derby, then stopped at various stations en route for the legendary resort. We worked this train as far as Nottingham, then crossed over the platforms to await 'The European', the boat train that ran up the Erewash Valley to Sheffield. Hauled by a Class 47 it was another good train to learn on.

As long as we did our work, Steve was happy to let us do our own thing during our days out. As we had a Manchester run-out coming up someone suggested a visit to the Coronation Street set. This started our Nottingham driver off about the temptations of Bet Lynch's chest. Steve was furious. Normally easy-going about most things he tore me off a strip for nattering while driving!

At Sheffield we had a quick cuppa and then went out for a Class 45 hauled express to Derby. I loved these locos, so I gave it my all whilst driving them. On other occasions we would work a Derby-Birmingham Peak-hauled service, nip round the flea market, then take another 45 to Sheffield, and yet a third one back down to Derby. My only regret is that although I kept a diary from day one, the pressures of taking my MP12 left me without enough time to keep as detailed a record as I would have liked. Many of the Peak workings remain only in my memory.

I enjoyed express work – it was certainly a change from coal trains! For me the best job was a St Pancras express which left Derby around 07.10 hauled by a double-headed Class 45. One was the booked engine for the train, the other on a test run after being in Derby works for a major overhaul. We only worked this job twice, but on both occasions I felt an immense sense of pride running in to London.

In the capital we'd have a quick snack and then spend a few hours sightseeing. I liked to head for Carnaby Street, but we tended to take turns choosing somewhere to visit. One day Steve wanted to go to a particular area, but as it was the end of the week Dean and I decided to head for home and left Steve to catch a later train. Unfortunately the one he got a cab ride off encountered a suicide near Leicester. As the driver was too upset, Steve had to go back down the track to inspect and mark the body. Suicide is always an awful and messy business and I shudder to think how we'd have felt if we'd been with Steve that day. Luckily we took that earlier train…

Over the years many horror stories have circulated the mess rooms. One often recounted in our area is about the driver who was running into Leicester Midland station. He'd done it hundreds of times before. But instead of the passengers edging forward, picking up their bags and cases, they all started to shrink back. A look of horror filled their faces as they pointed at the front of his engine. Women screamed and fainted at the sight of the decapitated body that hung from the hook on the front.

Another time a poor woman who had been in a mental hospital decided to end it all by jumping off a bridge in front of an oncoming express. Unfortunately she went straight through the middle window of a Class 45 and ended up between the driver and the second man on the floor of the cab.

Some drivers have experienced more than their fair share of horror. One of the nicest drivers at Coalville – sadly no longer with us – had the worst experience anyone could imagine. At Beeston Crossing a small boy trying to retrieve a ball got his hand caught between the road and the rail. The result was unbelievably awful to witness. One can't imagine what the driver must have gone through in the weeks and months following. After being off for months he came back and spent a long time working on shed. Eventually he agreed to go back on the main line and was sent on a refresher course to re-learn the routes. But then, unbelievably, he had another suicide – a man who looked the train crew straight in the eyes before he jumped.

That was it – it was too much for any man to bear – and the poor chap lasted only a short while longer on the railways after that.

We lost three good blokes that year whilst I was away on MP12. The irony is that someone had said 'I wonder if anything will happen while we're away.'

The first loss was Gordon Edwards, a good old boy who'd always keep you entertained with a tale or two. Apparently Gordon had just finished a week's conversion course on Class 58s. He had been passed out on the Friday before, then fell asleep in his armchair and never woke.

The other two deaths were just a coincidence. One was a good mate of mine, Nick Glover, a popular character who had just passed his MP12 and was doing conversions. On the Friday morning Dean had told us that Nick had been taken ill. We had no reason to think it was anything other than flu or a bad back or something. But after the weekend he came into the 4-shed messroom with terrible news: Nick had passed away. We were stunned into silence. A few Derby men lowered their voices and spoke in a low murmur. It was upsetting to think that a young man with so much to live for had been taken from us so quickly.

The other was ex Burton driver Jack Manley. Jack had died in the place where he'd spent his working life - on the railway. On an engine, in fact, on the shed. Jack and his mate were on night shed duties. They only had a couple of locos to get ready and agreed to do one each. After finishing his around 2.30 Nigel walked over to the shed side where Jack was preparing a Class 56.

'I've done that one, Jack,' he shouted up to the cab of the 56. 'I'll go and mash.'

'Good idea,' Jack called back. 'I'll be in as soon as I've done this.'

With that Nigel went off to the cabin. As he waited he chatted with the other blokes while he waited for Jack to come in. But Jack was taking ages. Nigel went back to the Class 56 to see what was keeping him. There was no answer to his shout, so he climbed up and opened the door. Something was wedged against it. Increasingly unnerved, Nigel went round to the other side and climbed in that way. There on the floor lay Jack. Nigel called his name, but there was no answer. Panicking now he ran back to the cabin to fetch help. But unfortunately it was too late.

The biggest coincidence was that Nick and Jack were renowned for their dislike of each other and many stories were told about their various spats. Though he had his good points, Jack was a hard man to get on with. Embittered by being permanently on shed due to illness, seeing young lads like Nick passing out for main line work was hard for him to bear. Nick was a young chap who lived life to the full and enjoyed his beer and motorbikes. He wouldn't suffer fools gladly and would never bow and scrape to those awkward older drivers like Jack.

23: The Training Train

For the rest of us the running out continued. We had to learn to handle air- and vacuum-braked freight and passenger trains. Also a loose-coupled freight with a brake van. We had done the passengers and now we would do the others.

A lot of handling would be learned on the training train, but the Derby men had got that so we had to wait. Steve said that whilst we were waiting we need look no further than our own depot. But we were slap-bang in the middle of the 1984 miner's strike and coal trains were few and far between. We'd had enough experience as second men and we wouldn't have touched one anyway due to the situation.

But we needed to brush up on our vacuum handling. For some reason our stone trains ran at night throughout that period, so we decided to work the West Drayton, a train which consisted of a 47 or a pair of 20s with a long rake of mineral wagons. It was an ideal train for us learn on, but it wasn't easy. Air-braking could be used how you liked, within reason, but vacuum techniques called for greater concentration. Not enough vacuum and nothing would happen - you either ran down a gradient or entered a speed restriction too quickly. But apply just a little too much and you'd almost come to a standstill!

'You haven't done bad for regular days,' said our conscientious but easy-going instructor. 'So we'll do a couple of night turns to get you on vacuum.'

At last we got our chance on the training train. The Leicester men had managed to hog it on days, so that meant us having it in the afternoons. Still, in my book, that was much better than nights.

This train consisted of a Class 25 or 31 and three of the dustiest broken-down coaches we had ever seen. Retrieved from the darkest corners of Etches Park they'd probably been there for years until someone decided to use them for driver training. The seats had been stacked up on top of each other and most of the glass was missing from the windows.

Our destination was Bedford, run round and back, simulating braking and handling at speed. We would then back it away for the evening along the wall sidings and take the engine back to the depot.

After a lunchtime shandy at the Merry Widows opposite Derby station we left at 14.00, just in time for the Leicester men to run the train round for us. Our train had to be accompanied by a regular train crew, so as we relieved the Leicester men our 'minders' walked by and climbed into the back cab. Once we were ready Steve went on the phone to the Derby power box to bell us out.

I had first go and enjoyed every minute of it. The 25 - or BoBo as many people still called them after their wheel arrangement - was a plucky little engine. I'd second-manned them but never actually driven one. With three coaches we soon got up to maximum speed. Along the route Steve chose various points approaching stations where we had to simulate braking. We weren't allowed to stop, just slow to 20-30 mph and then accelerate away.

'I know we can't actually stop,' I said. 'But why?'

'You'd get passengers trying to get on, of course!'

'You're pulling my leg.'

'You watch then. Slow right down at the next station.'

I did as asked. As we approached the platform I could see people getting off their seats, picking up their cases, shuffling towards the platform edge. Then we accelerated again and left them standing open-mouthed. To most folk a train is just a train, but they must have been shocked at the state of ours. They probably thought it was yet another sign of the British Rail's steady decline!

After running round at Bedford, Dean took the controls and enjoyed driving the 25 just as much as I had.

We were on class 31s for the rest of the week. One of them packed up on us halfway up Desborough Bank. Steve and the Derby driver quickly found the cause - the Woodward governor had come adrift - and they had to do a quick bodge job until a more permanent repair could be made.

Another day I got a nasty electric shock off the AWS reset button. This had to be pressed when passing over the magnet on the approach of a restrictive aspect (double or single yellow or red signal). If not reset, the brakes would automatically come on. Between Wellingborough and Kettering we received two restrictive aspects and again I got a jolt,

'I'm not touching that bloody thing again!' I protested.

'Just concentrate on your braking,' said Steve, 'and I'll cancel it.

He did so - but not before getting a jolt himself.

'I've got an idea,' I said. 'I'll use my orange vest.'

I tested it as we approached a red signal and it worked, so we were in business again. I went on the phone and the signalman informed us that we had a track circuit failure and we were to pass the signal at danger. So with one long blast of the horn - as laid down in the rule book - we set off again.

A couple of days later, after a trip to Bedford, we were standing at the signal opposite Derby Research Centre. I went down to the signal post telephone to tell the signalman we had arrived. As I turned back to our loco I noticed a large thick bar hanging off it. It turned out to be part of the brake linkage and could have caused untold damage or an accident to another train. After informing the power box we secured it temporarily until the loco got on shed for attention.

I rode back to Burton on a Class 45 with a Derby driver, a pleasant chap who asked how I was getting on with the MP12 course. At Burton we said goodbye. After the shrill whistle, the hiss of air brakes and a billow of blue smoke, the 'Peak' departed, taking its carriages into the distance.

Next day I was back at Derby and headed for the 4-shed mess room where we'd arranged to meet. Most of the regular train crews sat on the left side, while men from other depots sat on the right. Derby men - or HQ men as they were known - were a bit cliquey and wary of strangers, so I dropped my bag at a table on the right and settled down to await my instructor and fellow trainee. Across the table a driver was filling out his ticket - the same chap who'd given me a ride back on the 45. I greeted him cheerfully and he said hello. I was quite unprepared for what happened next. The murmur of conversation behind me stopped abruptly - followed by a silence so eerie that the hairs stood up on the back of my neck. One of the Derby lads I was on the course with came over from the other side.

'Come over here with us, Tony, ' he said. 'Don't be sitting with that f***ing scab.'

The driver just carried on filling in his ticket. Feeling pressurised I stood up, grabbed my bag and was more or less frog-marched to the other side of the cabin. The conversation started up again and everything returned to normal. The driver had apparently been one of those who worked during the 1982 strike. I'd always been proud to belong to ASLEF but this reaction seemed too extreme and I felt sorry for the man. I began to regret leaving that table but reluctantly decided that keeping my mouth shut was probably the best option.

By the middle of the following week our days on the training train were running out. I was in trouble with the parents of my girlfriend for taking her on a scooter rally at the weekend. She phoned me up and was almost too upset to tell me about it.

'Dad says money's no object - he's going to pay to have you taught a lesson.'

As if I didn't have enough things on my mind...

A couple of nights later I was out walking the dog when a car stopped alongside me. I could see four big blokes inside. The passenger side window was wound down and one beckoned me over.

'Hey mate, here.'

This is it, I thought. What should I do?

'Yes?' I said, tentatively approaching the car.

'Have you got a light?'

'Sorry, I don't smoke,' I replied, trying to sound as brave as I could.

'Okay, cheers then.'

With that they sped off. But it was still on my mind the next day when we met up in the Merry Widows pub. It was a real railwaymen's pub with a good crowd mixing there - inspectors, drivers, guards, second men. There was always a bit of good-humoured inter depot leg-pulling. Craig knew how to wind up the Derby men and used it with good results. I often wondered how we avoided a punch up - it certainly came close a few times! One day a Derby driver dropped a comment about our depot's involvement in the miner's strike. A few coal trains had been moved for various reasons and it was a subject we were all quite sensitive about.

I must have looked worried because Steve approached.

'You're very quiet, Tony. Is there something up?'

I shrugged it off and said it was nothing. But they kept on at me and in the end I decided to tell them.

'Sounds as if you've got a bit of a problem,' said Steve. 'I'd help if I could, but all I can say is try and put it at the back of your mind else it'll affect your driving.'

As we dropped down towards Bedford on our usual journey two military jets locked onto us. They were from a local airbase and regularly used that stretch of line for practise runs.

'They're just training,' said Steve. 'Beating us up - that's the RAF term for whenever they attack anything.'

Again the jets turned back on us and seemed so close and threatening.

'Hey,' said Steve, 'you don't think your girlfriend's dad has paid them to get you, do you?'

'I wouldn't put anything past him!'

We had to laugh. After that I began to treat my problem more light-heartedly. We reached Bedford safely (and not full of holes), ran round our train and the guard went back to carry out the brake test. A mixed engineering train driven by a Derby crew arrived on the adjacent platform. After being relieved by Bedford men they walked across to us.

'Are you going back to Derby?' they asked.

'Yes, shortly.'

'Can we ride back with you then?'

'Sure, but there's not much room. There's three of us up here and another three in the back cab.'

'It doesn't matter, we'll ride in the train.'

We all looked at each other and tried to warn them about the appalling condition of the carriages. But they were already walking down to them.

'It's their choice,' Steve said with a shrug.

The guard came back to ask if the brake test was OK and that he'd be in the back cab for the return journey. It was Dean's turn to drive, so I went down to the signal phone at the end of the platform to get us the road. As soon as the red turned to green off we went.

'Take her to the maximum,' Steve said to Dean. 'We'll give them Derby blokes a ride to remember!'

Dean did just that. By the time we reached Derby we'd forgotten all about our passengers. We were preparing to set back onto the goods line when all of a sudden Dean burst out laughing.

'Hey, just take a look at this lot!'

There were the three Derby men, their hands and faces black with dust, which our speed must have whipped up like a dust storm inside the carriages.

'Thanks a flaming bunch!' said one of the Derby men. 'Remind us not to ride in this thing again.'

'You shouldn't be allowed to run around with those at that speed,' their driver said. 'They're not running right. We thought we were coming off the road a few times.'

We couldn't help but smirk as they walked crossly away.

Two days later we were back to the classroom to recap and relax a bit. Points that had confused us were explained again. Things seemed to fall into place now and we worked hard from then on. We all wanted desperately to become train drivers and the MP 12 was our passport to that ambition. Only hard work could make our dreams reality. Failure would be such a humiliation. My greatest fear - and we all had it - was being the only one to fail while the rest of the trainees got through.

Our last day - a Friday - finally arrived. We'd eaten, slept and breathed rules and regulations and the workings of the class 47. Now the dreaded passing out ceremony was on us. An inspector was to take us all in turn for three days each. He was very keen, we were told. Most of them were, but some were worse than others.

'Right, that's it,' said Bernard, dismissing us at noon on our last day. 'I can't do any more for you now. Go off and get studying.'

We tried to get him to come for a pint with us, but he politely declined, pointing to a huge backlog of work. A few students took Bernard's advice and went home to start revising. For the rest of us, celebration was a priority and so we set off to enjoy a good afternoon in the Merry Widows.

24: Passing Out Week

The following Monday I was back at Coalville. I'd got used to being at Derby, but I'd missed our home depot and wanted to catch up on all the gossip. We began second-manning again while we awaited our passing out days out with the inspector.

It was late October and the inspector had already had some of our fellow MP12-ers in front of him. The Derby lot went first, then the Leicester men. Both lots passed. Our turn didn't come until mid December. Barry, the most senior of us, went first and got through, as did Dean and Craig soon after. Leaving just me. Word had got back to the LDC they were struggling to get an inspector and there was a possibility I might have to wait until after Christmas. Talk about unfair! The rest were all through and relaxed - but my Christmas would be spoiled by the worry, not to mention a head still chock-a-bloc with rules, regulations and engine data.

But my plight had been noted. One good thing about British Rail is that they tended to sympathise with their staff and if a problem could be sorted they would try their level best. After some juggling around an inspector was made available and he would come over to pass me out on Monday 17th. It made for a nervous weekend, but I was happy that it would soon be over one way or another. Revision became my priority. I made up my mind to spend Friday evening at it, but my resolve didn't hold. Saturday would do instead. But again I failed to knuckle down. If I didn't know it already then I never would. On Sunday night, though, I made a last-ditch effort and checked up on a few bits I was unsure of.

On Monday morning I attempted to enter the mess room quietly, but had to endure a fanfare of leg-pulling. The lads enjoyed seeing someone under pressure - especially as it was me - but all this teasing didn't help at all.

'Who's coming to see you today, Tony?'

'Hey, I've heard he's a real keen 'un.'

'Just mash him a cuppa and you'll be alright.'

I made a beeline for Craig and Dean who were also in there.

'What's he like?' I asked. 'What sort of things does he ask you?'

Before they had time to answer, an authoritative figure with a trilby and brown briefcase strode through the lobby into the TCS's office. I endured another round of teasing from the occupants of the mess room. A short while later the same man came to the door.

'Second man Tony Gregory please.'

I stood up nervously. What made it worse was the way some of the older men started chatting to him, while I just stood staring at the floor and wishing we could get started. In the conference room we settled ourselves down and made small talk about the weather and suchlike. Opening up his briefcase the inspector took out a sheaf of official looking papers and laid them carefully on the table.

'Shall we have a cup of tea before we start, Tony?'

I brewed up for us both, but I'd no sooner taken a sip of my tea when he began his interrogation. I got off to a bad start.

'Right, Tony, you are approaching a single - '

I don't know why he paused just then, and I wish he hadn't, else I wouldn't have said what I did.

'What, you mean a single yellow?'

'A single,' he repeated angrily.
It sounded just the same, but I quickly twigged. It seemed he couldn't pronounce the word signal properly, so it came out as single.

After that the questions came at a steady pace to begin with and were easy enough - but soon they came ever faster and ever more difficult. He was very keen and would not move on until he got an answer. But he was very patient with me and if I genuinely couldn't answer a question he would approach it from a different angle or give me some clues and then come back to it later. If I tried to bluff him, though, he would stare straight at me, as if he knew what I was up to. Perhaps he enjoyed putting young trainees under pressure. Or was he just doing the job he was paid for, making sure that trainees knew everything they should?

By lunchtime I felt washed out and went to mash up in the cabin. The other chaps were more sympathetic now and I had a quick morale-boosting chat with them before going back to the exam. George had taken a neat pack of sandwiches and began to eat them. I'd brought sandwiches too, but the strain of the day had taken away my appetite. I just sat and sipped my tea and tried to relax.

'Not hungry, Tony?' he said.

'Not really.'

'Oh, that's good,' he said, handing me some sheets of paper. 'You can show me how you would fill a report form in. Then a loco repair book. And then a driver's ticket.'

So while he sat there munching his sandwiches I ended up working through my lunch break. It wasn't that I minded missing my grub, just that I thought I had enough to do already without any extra. But I plodded on through the afternoon answering his questions. At ten to four he glanced at his watch.

'Is that the time already? We'd better pack up for the day - unless you want to do some more?'

I declined politely. He'd only been joking of course and sent me off home to prepare for another day's examination.

The next day was no easier. I had to describe fuel, water and oil systems, run through the electrical system, describe the layout of a Class 47 from the cab instruments to the engine room. We did preps and disposal and other topics. Finally another exhausting day drew to a close. At no time was I given a hint of how well I was doing. All he said was I was to meet up with him at 08.00 next day in the cabin at Derby 4-shed. I left for home, with a terrible headache, so fed up that I almost felt as if it no longer mattered if I passed or failed.

Next day Andy Clarke gave me a lift to Derby on the back of his motorbike. Andy and I had grown up together and he was now a second man at Derby. After a fast and scary ride we turned into Deadman's Lane and through the gates by the watchman's hut. Carrying on down the lane between Etches Park and the loco works, we arrived at the 4-shed booking-on point. I looked at the long lines of withdrawn and cannibalised locos, their blue liveries faded and scratched. Some were almost intact, but others had cabs or panels missing. Some were engine-less, others bore the dents and buckles of collision damage. The rails they stood on were red with rust. Silent and forlorn they awaited their final fate, the cutter's torch.

But there was no time to dwell on such things. Thanking Andy for the lift I went to report to the TCS.

'He'll meet you in the mess room,' he said. 'He's just sorting your trains out.'

I walked round to the cabin. Whatever happened now, at least it was the last day. The hardest part of the ordeal was now behind me. In fact, with the gruelling theory tests out of the way I was quite looking forward to the practicals. Once it was over I could start getting ready for Christmas. Walking into the mess room I got the usual indifferent looks from the Derby clique. Andy sat with a group of mates who were taking the mickey out of an old froggy-looking driver, calling him Baron von Greenback. I'd just started to tell Andy and his mates about the inspector's laughable way of saying 'single' instead of 'signal' when in he walked. I shut up quickly!

'Right, Tony,' said the inspector. 'It's your last day, so let's make a good one shall we?'

'I'll try,' I promised.

'Right then, your first job is a loose-coupled stone train from Chad to Leicester. We'll board it on the goods when it gets here.'

Our train consisted of two Class 20s, a long rake of stone hoppers and a guard's van way back in the rear. The driver opened the cab door for us and offered me the driver's seat.

'Sit down, Tony,' said George. 'Make yourself comfortable.'

The signal came off and George gave me the go-ahead. I released the brakes and eased open the power handle. Not too much or the poor old guard would get a mighty jolt. Rounding the tight curve of the goods road I saw that the junction signal was off for us. Taking care not to exceed the 10 mph limit I eased the controller back whilst looking behind to see that all was well.

Having someone looking over your shoulder all the time makes the job even harder to do, but I would just have to bear it. After a while the inspector took less notice of me and chatted with the driver. I felt better now, but I knew that he still had his eye on me. In those days inspectors were shrewd and conscientious chaps who had come up through the ranks. All they expected from you was that you did your job properly and safely and we had every respect for them.

I felt that I was doing well. But it takes a long time to get from Derby to Leicester with a Class 8 (maximum speed 35 mph!). Passing Trent Junction I started to get overcome by fatigue. The monotonous clickety-clack of the wheels and the early start to my day were taking their toll. My eyelids felt heavy and I fought to stay alert. Why today of all days! By Barrow-on-Soar though I perked up a bit and managed to stay the course until we were relived at Leicester. After thanking the Derby driver we went into the cabin for our break. Then we boarded a 45-hauled express to Nottingham. I drove the Peak without incident.

Our next move was a DMU back to Derby.

'You handled both of those trains very well,' the inspector confided during our journey.

I was pleased by his comments.

'But let's see how you do on a vacuum train,' he went on. 'We've got one for you. It's a daily tripper that leaves Derby St Mary's yard for Toton. It goes into Spondon yard to shunt, but not every day, it just depends.'

I knew of this tripper from the other trainees. He was trying to keep me guessing, but I knew that the others had all gone in and had to do quite a bit of shunting. In fact, I'd been told that it went in to Spondon nine times out of ten, so that's what I expected too.

We walked towards the goods line again to pick up our train, a mixed freight, with a Class 25 pulling coal trucks, tanks, flat, ballast wagons and a brake van. Most were destined for the wagon shops. I checked the driver's slip and waited for the signal. The second man went on to the phone then he and the driver retired to the back cab. The signal came off and the little 25 chugged slowly round the goods line curve.

'You're lucky today, Tony,' said the inspector. 'We're not going into Spondon, we're right away.'

The journey went without incident and as we approached Long Eaton he told me to stop at the end of the platform.

'This is as far as we go, Tony.'

He pressed the firebell to alert the crew to relieve us. I gently applied the brakes and stopped neatly at the platform end. The crew took over and after exchanging farewells we watched the train head towards Sheet Stores Junction. The wagons squeaked and clanged their way past us, leaving us in silence broken only by the whistling of birds. The inspector opened his briefcase and began to scribble down notes. My butterflies returned with a vengeance. Not more questions! The inspector never uttered a word. I was sure I had failed and I just couldn't rid myself of the black thoughts. All of a sudden he stabbed at his paper, adding his last full stop with a flourish. Putting the top back on his pen he broke into a smile.

'Well, Tony, we've come to the end of your MP12 examination and I must say that you've done very well. I'm pleased to say that you've reached the required standard. And so we must now make a driver of you.'

With that he held out his hand and shook mine. I could only just stammer out my thanks. It had been a long time since the beginning of May and I could hardly believe what I'd just heard.

'Well, I've done with you now, Tony,' he said. You can toddle off home or do whatever you have to do. Again, well done, and all the best for your future on the railway.'
I thanked him again and we took our leave of each other. I made my way down the slope under the bridge and onto the opposite platform to await my train home. Now that the shock had worn off I wanted to tell everyone my news.

Mum and Dad were overjoyed. They knew how much it meant to me. But I was exhausted by it all. After dinner I went straight to bed and slept like I'd done a week of nights!

A nice relaxing Christmas came and went, thanks to those who'd found that inspector for me so late in the day. On the 29th of January I went for my compulsory medical, but apart from that it all remained quiet and the four of us went back to second-manning.

Very much how it always was - fun and contentment was on the cards for this bunch of Coalville drivers. Photo: John Oldershaw.

25: Relief Drivers

The four successful MP12 candidates were asked to book on at 08.00 on Wednesday 13th February 1985 to be issued with new equipment, fill in various forms and be assessed by Rex Wilcox, the Derby-based train crew manager.

We went in pairs, Craig and Barry, then Dean and I. After congratulating us, Rex gave us a pep talk about pride in the job and keeping our noses clean. He also gave us twenty good reasons why we should be moving coal. Most drivers were then blacking it because of the miner's strike. Then he shook us by the hand, wished us all the best and confirmed our status as passed men or relief drivers. Although we hadn't yet done a route card and were passed only on Class 47s, we were issued with a new driver's bag, plus a BR issue T-key (better known as a carriage key) and a desk key which would unlock the controls of nearly all BR locos.

Five weeks later we did our first week-long conversion course to other loco classes. Class 20s or Type 1s were first. This old BR workhorse was first produced in 1957 at the Vulcan foundry and proved so dependable that the last one came into service as late as 1967. With their 8-cylinder 1000 hp engines the 20s would never break any records, but they soldiered on at a steady pace and rarely failed. I enjoyed the conversion to this class, as they were so basic.

Our next loco - the new-ish class 56 - was quite different. Circuit breakers and different electrical systems made them much more technical. We had the same instructor on all three conversions at Coalville. He was good, but perhaps a little too keen. The Derby inspector was just the opposite and once he knew we were clued-up he was satisfied. Friday was always passing out day and in the engine room, after Dean had answered the first question, he said:

'Right, Tony, your question next. What time does the Snibstone Inn open?'

We were quite taken aback. We looked at one another and then at our watches.

'Now,' we said.

'Right, do you fancy finishing off up there then?'

We jumped at the chance. Friday was always a good day at the Snibby as the place was full of Coalville railwaymen. The inspector filled in our competence tickets in the bar.

A few days later we were told to fill in our route cards. These large folded cards have all the routes and depot locations printed on them and we were asked to sign the roads we were confident on. As passed men we were able to sign most of the local routes. This doubled your chances of getting a driving turn and if you got one you'd be on a rate of pay close to that of a registered driver.

Most men kept a diary of their driving turns, for once you had attained a hundred you would then go on to a higher rate of pay. My sign denoting a driving turn was a black asterisk circled in red. My first official turn was down to Charlie Farren. Having taken some locos to Toton on the 07.00 ferry, we were then required to bring back 47204 light engine. Due to problems on the Stenson branch we were told to return to Coalville via Derby. Luckily I'd already signed the road and Charlie had a refresher for the route.

'Here you are, Tony,' he said. 'You can conduct me that way and get your first driving turn in.'

It was a joke really: Charlie knew the road better than I did. But if a driver hasn't been over a route for a while he would put in for a review and would be sent on a refresher as soon as it was possible. That trip really gave me a taste for driving and I wanted more. But for the next couple of weeks I had to be content with second man's turns, which now seemed quite menial!

My next chance came on the 23rd April. We were now learning the Class 58. Fifty of these powerful (and complicated!) machines had been built by BREL at Doncaster. Compared to the class 20's 1000 hp these locos had a staggering 3300 hp. The 58 had been built very much with the driver in mind. A corridor between the cab and the engine cut down noise and the cabs were draught-proofed, making for a very comfortable environment. Whilst in the classroom doing the systems, our TCS came in and told us that a 58 was standing at Toton waiting to come to Coalville. No drivers were available to fetch it and as Toton men hadn't learned the branch then we'd have to go and collect it.

'Sorry, can't oblige,' said our instructor. 'I've put in a refresher for Trent Junction to Toton.'

Here was my chance. I'd already signed that road, so I said I'd happily conduct him on the road if he conducted me on the traction. I wasn't sure if he'd like it - an instructor being conducted by some young relief driver - but we did it and driving turn No.2 was in the bag!

Some of the older railwaymen regarded relief drivers as the lowest of the low, an upstart who would resort to any tricks to get a driving turn. There was an element of truth in it, but mostly it was just messroom banter. After all, the old hands had all been passed men once and they knew what it was like. Indeed, many would go out of their way to help you get a driving turn.

The author couples class 20s to failed 37 at Gresley in 1985, accompanied by instructors John Kenny and Derby's Dick Swift and Coalville driver Malc Goulding
Photo: Rob Woodman

On the 10th of May I had my first driving turn without being accompanied by a qualified driver. It was the 06.20 Rugeley. I'd second-manned the job all week, but as they were desperate for drivers, I was given the job. I shared the driving with my second man, as usual. It didn't feel any different really, but this time I was responsible.

That was my third turn. The driver's slip issued to me on that day is still in my possession.

As the weeks went by the turns increased. Sometimes I would get a whole week at a time, other weeks just the odd one. Sometimes a registered driver or another passed man would be booked on a turn that was, technically, your job. And so a claim went in. You proved this by showing the roster clerk your diary entry for that date. That's why most railwaymen kept a diary and all three unions - ASLEF, NUR and TSSA - still issue them to their members.

26: Long-Forgotten Fun

Not long ago, whilst talking to old Coalville mate - Tony Ellison - I was reminded of some of the pranks that used to go on every day. Tony was sidekick to the ever-playful Gary Middleton, a chap who wouldn't pause for a moment before playing a prank. Both were tappers (or Rolling Stock Technicians as they are dubbed today). Together they were lethal. But what a happier railway it was then...

One Christmas I wanted some holly so I asked Tony & Gary where I could get some.

'Bardon,' they told me. 'There's trees there laden with the stuff. We're going up there in half an hour to examine the 'Hayes'. You can ride in the back of the van.'

I'd been 06.00 shed and the bulk of the work had been done, so I asked my mate if I could go.

'Yes,' he said, looking up from his game of cards. 'Off you go.'

For the next forty minutes I was on the ride to hell and back. Even at Bardon they drove around at breakneck speed on heaps of ballast, throwing me around like a pea in a tin, hitting the sides and roof. But I got some cracking holly branches.

I certainly had my share of their torments. Once, whilst I was out on a job, they managed to open the door of my mini and push it into the old wooden goods shed with the aid of a ramp they'd made from two sleepers. Then they slammed the doors shut. I came back and - panic! - no car. I dashed to the office to ring the police, but I was halfway through dialling when I heard the tittering behind me!

Another time they opened the bonnet and took the caps off my spark plugs, replacing them gently on top so it looked like they were properly in place. The result was obvious. Another time I drove home blissfully unaware that they'd tied a pair of lady's briefs to the front grille.

They weren't choosy about who they played up. Bob Arnold was another prime target. Bob had been a shunter at Drakelow but was transferred to Coalville as a cleaner. Bob wasn't the sharpest knife in the drawer and never took the time to think things out -, as was the case when the front brake hub of his motorbike developed a squeak. He was quite right to fetch an oilcan from the stores, but things went wrong when he used it. He was so pleased to cure the squeak - but not so pleased when the oily brakes failed to stop him and he came a cropper in the hedgerow.

With the bike gone Bob walked from his home in Burton to Coalville every day, a distance of 17 miles each way! One wet Monday morning the poor soul got soaked to the skin - only to be informed on his arrival that he should have been on annual leave! Taking pity, me and some of the other blokes started giving him a lift.

Bob was a dream gull for Garry and Tony. They had so much fun at his expense. Some of their jokes were prolonged - like the time they sawed an inch off the handle of his sweeping brush every day until he was almost bent double trying to use it.

A few weeks later he nipped up to Coalville town to fetch two pints of milk. The two tappers quietly nipped in behind him and pulled down his trousers so that Bob stood there with his hands full and his kecks around his ankles.

When he was on the loo once they went out and blew down the cistern overflow pipe. A loud trumpeting sound filled the cubicle and a panicky Bob shot out of the door with his pants and trousers still around his ankles. Another loo trick was to stretch cling film over the toilet bowl, with obvious results for the unobservant. The best of their toilet tricks was when they carefully placed an old pair of boots in one of the cubicles and draped a pair of old overall bottoms over them. Locking the door from the inside, they then climbed out over the top. Right on cue, the cleaner arrived and began her duties. She cleaned all the other cubicles but couldn't get into the rigged one. Peering under the gap she saw the boots and overalls and tapped on the door.

'Excuse me,' she called, 'I've got to clean in there.'

Getting no reply, she rushed off to the office to report that someone was either asleep or dead on the toilet!

Another victim was Coalville driver Bo Farmer. After nipping to the market to get his week's groceries he made the mistake of bringing them into work. The shopping bag was too tempting a target for Gary and Tony. Nothing was damaged or stolen, but they actually added an extra item - a large piece of rail wrapped in greaseproof paper. Nothing was said about it for a week or so.

'Hey Bo, did you open that greaseproof paper that was in last week's shopping?' asked one of the jokers.

'No, why? It's still in the fridge.'

One of the Coalville shunters would often take home a bag of coal, spillage picked up from around the sidings, an unofficial perk that provided him with a fair bit of free heating. It was a heavy load for him to carry, but he thought the savings well worth it. One day the terrible twosome tipped out all the coal from his bag and replaced it with ballast, topping it off with a couple of inches of real coal so that the poor soul wouldn't suspect. The shunter then struggled all the way home with a bag of useless ballast!

Another victim was Roy Storer, our long-suffering roster clerk, pay clerk and general clerical dogsbody. While working busily one day Gary and Tony managed to rig up a length of fishing line from Mantle Lane box across to our booking-on point. It was attached to a board at the top of the building just above Roy's window. From this hung another bit of line with a button attached. A complex set-up, but they thought it well worth it for the fun they were about to have. With each tug on the line came a tap on Roy's window. The poor man kept getting up and looking out - but there was no one to be seen. How long they carried on I don't know, but the poor man must have been well flummoxed!

Whilst examining a train in Mantle Lane they were suddenly aware of something approaching Coalville on the up line. It wasn't an empty stone or coal train but a medium-sized horse! They tried to get the beast out of the 'four foot' (space between the rails) but it just plodded on its merry way. A block was put on both lines but eventually it ended up in Halfords car park.

The photocopier was always useful for fun, messing about with photos of colleagues and sticking their heads onto preposterous bodies. We even copied a £10 note, stuck it in a pay packet with a payslip and left it on the floor of the lobby. It looked quite real and we had plenty of fun tricking the depot workers with it. But I'll give them their due - even though we tricked them into thinking they'd found a wage packet they all handed it in. The only rogues were two S & T men. One spotted it, nudged the other, then had it away in a flash. We had to tap on the window of their van to retrieve it. Had it really been someone's wages they would have been gone for good!

The fax machine also came in for some stick. Gary would inhale a lungful of smoke from one of his habitual cigars and blow it into the fax machine. Then he'd walk off innocently to the other side of the room.

'Look at the bloody fax,' he'd cry. 'There must be something up with the bugger!'

Many's the person who got caught by this trick and rushed to switch the machine off at the plug. People's heads also got the same treatment. If any chap had thick hair it would take a while for the long wisps of smoke to start escaping from his thatch. The poor devil would wonder what was up as he walked into the cabin and everyone fell about. But the trick went wrong once when they did it to our long-suffering TCS. Gary pretended to flick ash onto his turban - but then it was panic stations as the turban started to smoulder for real. After a couple of minutes trying to flick the ash off, they eventually succeeded with a bit of paper. But the smouldering continued until one of them flicked some water at it. Nothing could be done about the hole though!

One New Year I went to a fancy dress party as a soldier. The uniform and webbing were authentic, borrowed off Ian Carder, an ex Coldstream Guard. The helmet was Second World War 'tommy' style. I had a tommy gun, which I'd made out of wood and it looked real enough

Railwaymen in jovial mood alongside classes 08,31 and 20 in Mantle Lane Sidings 1977.
Photo: Steve Marks.

from a distance. After the party, for a bit of fun, I took the gun into work with me. Gary and Tony soon liberated it from me to use in one of their tricks.

Our Polish shunter had a keen interest in WW2 stuff and we made a point of standing alongside the building, acting as if we were trying to hide As soon as he spotted us we pretended to hide the gun and scurry away. After repeating the pantomime several different places he took the bait.

'What is it you are doing with that gun you have?'

'What gun? We haven't got a gun.'

'Hey,' he said angrily. 'You think I am blind? I saw you with it. It was a machine gun.'

It was hard to keep a straight face but somehow we managed it.

'No, you won't fool me,' he said sternly, tapping his nose and putting his cigarette holder in his mouth.

Once we had his attention again we knelt down and pretended to aim it. I must say it looked realistic with its brown wooden butt and long vertical magazine. And that's how it went. He kept coming back over the boards and we kept hiding it. We never did tell him it was only a bit of wood!

In the late 1980s car technology had finally reached Coalville. One of the younger second men bought a sporty little car and on it was the latest in car alarms. With the push of a button the car could be locked and unlocked by remote control and the indicators and headlights would flash. Chargeman Ivor Haskett peered through the messroom window just as the car's owner was showing off.

'Who's messing about inside that car? Someone's flashing the headlights.'

It was a golden opportunity for trickery! Several times we had Ivor going out to try and catch the mysterious culprit - but by the time he reached the car it was always locked and, of course, there was no one around. He had great fun with his gadget, activating the alarm again as soon as Ivor returned from his vigilante role.

Amongst the comic tricksters once based at Coalville was little Geoff Crowder. Geoff was a real character. He had quite a sense of humour and would often do things that others wouldn't dare to. One evening Geoff and I took some engines to Leicester for fuel and water. Walking into the mess room we found a group of Leicester men glued to a Leicester City match on TV. The volume was up so loud that there wasn't much chance of a chat. As the game reached fever pitch Geoff picked up the remote.

'What's this button for?' he asked innocently.

You'd have had to be there to appreciate the reaction - the yells and the curses those men came out with was atrocious. But it didn't stop there. After things had settled down again Geoff put a few coins in the one-armed bandit (most messrooms had them to help finance the welfare fund). The greedy machine had soon gobbled up his change. He then took out a bunch of keys and dangled them in the cash tray. With steady wrist movements he made a sound not unlike large handfuls of coins falling out after a jackpot. Again the Leicester men were distracted from their game.

'How much you won mate? What you got then?'

With a smile Geoff pulled out his keys. The men aimed angry glares in his direction before turning back to the game. How we managed to get out of that messroom alive I'll never know!

Some weeks later we arrived at Christmas week. I had been on earlies and was about to leave for home when Geoff Crowder and guard Graham Cross booked on to conduct Derby men into Drakelow. Knowing that I lived near Burton station Geoff asked if they could pop round later for a Christmas drink with my then girlfriend and me.

'Of course you can,' I replied - assuming it was just a joke!

But come teatime there was a knock on the door and there stood the two railwaymen.

'You said to nip in for a drink,' they said.

'You'll never guess what Geoff did while we were waiting for the Derby men in the platform office,' said Graham. 'The chargeman went out to get a train away and Geoff only pushed the button for the Tannoy and started singing Jingle Bells. Everyone on the platform was looking up at the speakers!'

In those days it was still a rule that staff must never drink while on duty. But it was generally ignored so long as blokes kept it moderate. As most did. We decided to nip for a quick pint and game of cards at my local before they went back to the depot. A pleasant time was had by all but it was all too soon time to leave. We arrived home to find that someone had locked the keys in the door so we had to borrow a ladder from next door and go in through the upstairs window. Towards the top of the ladder I was starting to get nervous and began to climb down again. Graham was made of sterner stuff however.

'Step aside. If you daren't do it I will.'

He scaled the ladder and attempted to climb through the top window. The noise started my Labrador barking and jumping all over the place. Then as Graham eased his large frame through the window the dog recognised him and started to lick his face. With both arms trapped Graham could do nothing but struggle.

'I'm bloody stuck!'

Then the two kicking legs disappeared inside, accompanied by a loud tearing sound and an almighty thud. After a while the back door was opened and Graham stood there. We couldn't stop laughing. The window catch had ripped his railway trousers from the ankle to the inside of his thigh! They ordered a taxi from Burton station and bade us farewell. I was still laughing as I watched them walk away, with Graham's bare leg and torn trousers flapping in the wind!

27: The Miners' Strike

The miners' strike started exactly a week after we began our MP12. The railways were not directly involved at that time and didn't become so until March when ASLEF and the NUR along with other unions decided to support the NUM by imposing a block on coal movements.

Coalville depot, like many others, was soon in the thick of it. Although the four of us were on our MP12 at Derby we followed developments eagerly. It wasn't just the politics of the strike itself, but we wondered how our mates at the depot would react to being involved. As we talked it over it soon became clear that we were all in support of the strike and greatly admired the miners and their families. Not everyone felt the same, of course, but even those who didn't ought to acknowledge the courage of ordinary working people taking on the might of the Thatcher government. No one had any idea how long it would go on for. Some said it would end in victory for the miners - as it had in 1972 - others said they would get a well-deserved comeuppance.

My only memory of the 1972 strike was visiting a sweet shop with a mate whose dad was a striking miner. The shopkeeper, who we knew well, told my pal that his dad should be put against the wall and shot - a vile comment that should never have been addressed to two innocent children. I'd always remembered those words and the way they were said. We were to hear many similar remarks over the weeks to come.

Men at our depot knew as far back as 1983 that something was brewing. We couldn't stock up the power stations quickly enough. Drakelow's stockpile was so big that it kept catching fire deep inside due to combustion. Huge earthmovers were brought in to keep moving and spreading the coal about day and night. As space ran out at Rugeley power station the perimeter access road was covered in thousands of tons of coal. It seemed as if a plan was being prepared - a plan for confrontation.

In April 1984 the first railwaymen were sent home for refusing or blacking the coal. Some of them would not move a coal train for the rest of the year-long dispute. Donations from organisations and unions in support of the miners were partially used to pay train crews for loss of earnings when they were sent home. BR would not pay for refusal to work. A few drivers and guards decided to work the coal trains. It wasn't really a railway dispute, they said. Anyway, when did the miners ever help the railwaymen, they asked. Where were they in '82 when we needed help and support?

Whilst at Derby station one group of Yorkshire miners were collecting donations and outlining their case to the public. We stood and watched for a while, noting that they received more sympathy than scorn. A couple of them came over with a bucket. As we chucked some money in one of them noticed our badges.

'Hey, look lads, they're ASLEF men.'

They shook our hands and asked if we were boycotting coal trains too. We explained that we were still training but we made our feelings known.

'It could still be going on a long time after you've finished.'

With that one of the miners unpinned his NUM badge and dropped it into my hand, thanking us before disappearing in the crowds.

The Derby branch of ASLEF brought in a large box and invited depot workers to bring tins of food for striking miners and their families. One night some spiteful saboteur ripped off all the labels from the tins.

At the end of December all the MP12-ers went back to their home depots. Almost immediately I was asked to second man a coal train. My refusal brought scorn to the face of the TCS.

'You're like sheep, you lot, all following the others.'

'You're wrong,' I said. 'We've got minds of our own and we stick to our principles.'

'Right, I can't use you then. See you tomorrow.'

This became a regular occurrence. On nights we were regularly stopped by police looking for flying pickets coming down from Yorkshire. Sometimes they simply looked in the car and asked what your business was at such a late hour. When I told them where I worked some got quite obnoxious with me. Coalville depot was well-known for its support of the miners. Signalmen were also blacking coal trains and a local MP even accused one of being mentally unstable for refusing to pull off his signals. Coal bound for hospitals was allowed to travel though.

In the Coalville area a small group of miners - known as the Dirty Thirty - stayed out for the duration. They had to put up with considerable violence and abuse from working miners. It was almost as if they were the blacklegs! They sometimes came to meetings or down to the depot and were given a warm welcome by most blokes. A handful of South Derbyshire men also stayed out for the duration, which again was an act of courage in my books.

During the first weeks of 1985 the strike began to crumble. We'd stuck by the miners, but were undermined by thousands of greedy lorry drivers. Anything that would carry coal was being used and these trucks thundered through the area day and night for days on end. And so the coal got through.

A vote on Sunday 3rd March brought the dispute to an end and two days later they marched proudly back to work beneath their banners. I watched the emotional spectacle on the news before setting off to work for the 14.00 shed.

But the bitterness was to linger for a long time. One morning I said hello to one of my favourite old hand drivers.

'You're not supposed to talk to me any more Tony,' he said.

He'd moved coal, but only done his basic eight-hour shift and not a minute more. I told him not to be silly. Once he knew I bore him no malice he relaxed.

'Tell you what then, we'll both have placards with GOOD MORNING on them.'

We both laughed. There were some drivers I could never fall out with, but some regarded their acts as unforgivable.

Later in the year railwaymen from Coalville were invited to Kersley Colliery Miners Club near Coventry. We filled a 52-seater coach and were present to see the unveiling of a painting of a railwayman shaking hands with a miner. Called up onto the stage we were given a standing ovation. The event was charged with emotion, the like of which I'd never experienced before or since.

20143 and 20141 partly derailed and embedded in the earth at Mantle Lane West in 1984. The locos came to grief while hauling a rakc of HAA wagons down the No1 reception, known locally as 'The Lickey'.
Photo: John Tuffs.

28: First Incident

The 19th June 1985 was destined to be a gloriously hot summer's day. I was at peace with the world as I strolled to my loco for the day - 58024. As I put in the battery and lighting switches I looked upwards to listen to a skylark as it whistled in the skies above. The sun quickly warmed my face. I'd booked on at 08.50, enjoyed the company in the mess room and sipped at a cuppa until my booked time off shed.

'I'll meet you over there, Tony,' said the guard.

Now young and keen I sounded the horn and slowly made my way to the departure dolly to bell out. It was already my eighth driving turn. As I waited for the signalman to answer the phone I looked back at the engine shining in the sun. Suddenly a negative thought came into my mind. Now I was driving nearly every day, my chances of having an accident or derailment were greatly increased.

Ten minutes later I was off the road!

I'd done everything by the book - changed ends at the right place and awaited the chargeman's signal to allow me into the yard.

'The road's set for you Tony to drop onto your train,' said chargeman Ivor Haskett.

Stopping a little over six feet off the wagons, as was the ruling, I went to ease the engine up to the wagons. Suddenly there was a loud bang beneath the loco. In those vital seconds inexperience told me to take no action until I had buffered up. Once that was done I jumped down to check both bogies. Ivor and another shunter came running.

'We heard the bang - what the heck was it?'

We checked the wheels, but all were firmly on the road. Looking closer we realised what had happened: the road itself had spread and the first bogie had been derailed. Had I braked on hearing the bang we'd have stopped off the road, but by letting her go that little bit more she had re-railed herself again. The signs were obvious - broken sleepers and chairs lay scattered in abundance.

After informing the TCS and promising to fill in a report later, I was given the next train on the up in order to carry on with my shift. That loco was 58019, which was fated to suffer a much worse derailment in the not-too-distant future. 58024 was trapped on her train all day as the platelayers worked in the overbearing heat to get her free. The rest of the day passed uneventfully and as I got relieved on the boards the gangers had about finished their work.

The next day, when Ivor Haskett came into the cabin and saw me he started to laugh.

'That was strange, you dropping off the road like that and then re-railing. But you wouldn't be the first. A steam loco did the same thing many years ago, and not far from where you came off either.'

My tally of driving turns increased week by week and I ended the year with thirty three to my credit. By January 1986 the Midlands was blighted by heavy snow showers and severe frosts. On the night of the 7th I was 20.10 spare. I'd managed to get through from Burton but many of the lorry drivers using the A50 had got stuck in deep snowdrifts. Some were almost covered! The railways fared no better: nothing could get on or off shed due to the points clogging up. With the P-way gangs busy elsewhere, those of us who'd made it to work got ourselves wrapped up and set to work with shovels. We got one or two cars out for men who were trying to get home, and then we attempted to clear the points so that locos were able to come onto the shed. The weather was getting worse. Our TCS said that anyone with a distance to go should set off for home while the roads were still passable. I left at 22.15. After several turnarounds and diversions I finally made it.

The next day was not so bad. Though there was still plenty of snow on the ground, the snow wasn't falling so heavily. I booked on at 18.00 and was given a driving turn straightaway - Coalfields Farm to Drakelow C station. The guard was also from Burton, the son of an old teacher of mine. Steve had spectacles like the bottom of milk bottles and even with them on he seemed to have difficulty seeing much. We all pulled his leg about it, but he didn't mind too much.

At Coalfields we loaded the train. It was dark and bitterly cold with a sharp frost threatening. Whilst running round I dropped Steve at the Hugglescote frame, then carried on over the points. He would then work the frame for me to proceed onto the other end of the train. I acknowledged his white light with a toot and went forwards. As I passed the frame he stepped down to watch me over - then all of a sudden his Bardic lamp flew into the air and a spread-eagled figure disappeared down the steep bank, arms and legs flailing. I stopping the Class 20s and ran back towards him. Shining my Bardic in his general direction I saw a black mass in a railway greatcoat rolling about in a thick snowdrift. He had slipped and rolled down, losing his hat and glasses on the way. Every time he tried to climb back up he just slipped back down. Eventually he got high enough to grab my hand and I pulled him up. I was laughing so much so that I nearly went tumbling down on top of him. He managed to retrieve his lost items and I dusted the snow off him.

We weren't destined to have much luck that day. As we reached Drakelow the speed module blew up while we were unloading, so we backed the train onto the middle road and went back light engine to Coalville.

29: Moods and Habits of the Train Driver

By the summer of 1985 I realised what great strides I'd made towards my boyhood ambition of being a train driver. In just over six years too. The old boys said that a man might take twenty or thirty years as a fireman before he got a chance to become a driver. There'd even been some who reached retirement age before they'd had a chance of being made up to drivers.

Now, as Coalville's youngest relief driver, I seemed to have the best of both worlds: still second manning, but often getting a chance to do some real driving.

The depot's old hands were a grand bunch, but they had some funny ways. Dennis Kendrick was an easy-going sort and let you get away with things that others wouldn't - like taking a nap or putting your feet up in the cab. He struggled from cab to cab with his bag, Bardic lamp, coat and smock (which I never saw him use). Not long after I started, whilst on a trip to Coalfields Farm, I'd commented to a driver about the amount of empty Woodbines packets strewn around under Forest Road bridge.

'Somebody's probably raided a machine,' he guessed, though he was as puzzled as I was. 'Emptied all the fags out then dumped the packets here.'

It seemed a likely explanation. A few days later I was passing under the same bridge again - this time with Dennis. As we went through he opened the cab window, pulled a handful of Woodbine packets from his pocket and threw them out.

'So you're the culprit!' I exclaimed. 'Why do you do that, Dennis?'

'Dunno,' he chuckled. 'Just habit I suppose.'

In time perhaps we younger ones would develop funny habits of our own. I suppose I already had some - like messing about and generally being a nuisance. A prime example is the morning when Cyril Kendrick and I left Toton with a light engine 58. Cyril had been pulling my leg in front of everyone in the mess room and I'd decided to get revenge. As I drove back he put his feet up and was soon asleep, shaking the cab with his deep throaty snores. Seeing that his feet were just inches away from the hotplate, for devilment I switched on the heat. We were approaching Burton-on-Trent before I decided not to be so horrible and turned it off. Two yellow signals slowed us down for Leicester Junction, but then we suddenly got a green and the junction indicator for the branch. As I accelerated I forgot all about poor Cyril - until I smelled the burning. Cyril suddenly shot to his feet.

'What the bloody hell...'

As smoke from his melting shoes filled the cab I started to regret my joke. He was going to go mad at me!

'You daft bugger, look at my shoe! You could have set me alight.'

'Sorry,' I said, trying not to snigger. 'It was meant to be a joke.'

A half-inch rut had been burned into his heel. You should have seen his walk as he headed back to the messroom. He couldn't say a lot, though, as he was always messing about himself.

Another time a mate of mine silver-soldered a 10p coin to a nail and when the cabin was empty I hammered the coin tightly down onto the shedman's bench. After a while the cabin began to fill up and eventually Cyril sauntered in. Now Cyril's favourite things, in order, were probably his money, his beer and his cards, so when a card school was suggested he went to sit down

'That's mine,' he said when he saw the 10p.

I tried to keep a straight face as he tugged at the stubborn coin.

'Ouch!' he said, 'I've broken me bloody nail now.'

Cards, horse-racing and dogs were all favourite topics of conversation with drivers. Some, however, were more conscientious and liked nothing better than to sit discussing rules, regulations and engines. In the old days railwaymen had MIC (mutual improvement classes) which they would attend once a week to improve themselves. By this time such things were long gone, but unofficial MICs were still held in many a mess room up and down the country.

While the older men had had their enthusiasm dampened by years of hard work, some of the younger ones were still obsessed by the railways, as illustrated by the time when an old hand driver and his mate passed a scantily-clad lady on the platform at Leicester.

'Wow, that's nice isn't it?' said the driver, ogling the view.

'Yes, she's lovely,' agreed his mate, eyeing up a Class 47 that simultaneously crept onto Beal Street shed. 'Just out of Crewe works, you know.'

Other drivers were renowned for their mood swings, of which we younger men often bore the brunt. Autumn 1985 saw me involved with a real corker! All week I had second-manned the 12.50 Coalfields Farm - Landor Street, bound for Didcot. The week went by like clockwork and the driver, guard and I had an excellent rapport. Up until Thursday that is. The first thing to go wrong was that no engine or train of empties was available, so we would have to wait for a set arriving at Coalville. Another crew were in front of us, so it would have to be the second train for us.

'It would happen today,' I grumbled. 'Thursday is my night out.'

'I've got relatives staying over,' the driver told me. 'I want to get home as soon as I can.'

But two hours passed before we relieved our train on the up line. From bitter experience we knew that if something went wrong early in the shift then things were bound to go wrong all day. So we weren't surprised when we arrived at Coalfields and the dolly stayed on. When they had coal it would be off ready for you to begin loading - but not that day. Our guard went to the control room and was told it would be another hour before they had enough coal for us. The driver's mood went rapidly downhill from then on - he was nothing like the same chap who'd been so jolly all week!

'We'll be too late to go soon, Bill,' I said, trying to test the water.

Instead of replying he just stared moodily through the windscreen. Time ticked by and I decided that if I was going to get my night out I'd have to ask for relief at Coalville. No longer a callow 17-year-old, I felt that I was almost a proper driver and quite capable of making such decisions for myself.

'I'm going to ask the TCS for relief. It's too late to go through with it now and he'll have plenty of men in the cabin this time of night.'

'Not for me you're not,' the driver said, downright angry now.

Despite his response I went off to phone the TCS from the lineside phone.

'Yes, stop on the boards,' he said 'and I'll send someone out for you.'

I'll never understand what followed. The driver had a chance to finish at a reasonable time and get home - yet he stubbornly insisted on going through with it. The dolly eventually came off and once loaded we ran round and the guard went back to do the brake test. The driver then broke the silence.

'So you've asked for relief have you?'

'Yes.'

'Not for me I hope.' He seemed to be spoiling for a confrontation.

'No.'

'Has he got someone then?'

'He's sending some relief when we get to Coalville.'

The driver was absolutely livid. With his next statement he forfeited and lost the argument.

'Right, I'll tell you now Tony - if there's a green 'un at the crossing you're going through whether you like it or not.'

I looked at him in disbelief: it had now gone beyond a joke. Again I attempted to reason with him.

'Come on, don't be silly. You know you can't take me through against my will. Anyway, I wouldn't let you.'

Not being the type to fall out with anyone unless I had to, I hoped he would now accept that I was dropping off at Mantle Lane. The guard stepped into the cab and must have noticed the atmosphere.

'Brake test OK,' he said.

A moody nod was all he got in reply, so he handed Bill the driver's slip and skedaddled into the back cab. We left the branch and approached the crossing. I was now calm and ready for whatever happened next. I put my coat on, picked up my bag and waited. The barriers dropped and all the signals went to green. As I expected he opened her up.

'Are you dropping me off?'

'I told you what I was going to do,' he said.

My stomach tensed. I had put a stop to this nonsense once and for all. Livid though I was, I spoke clearly and politely.

'Right, I will warn you once. If you don't shut off and apply the brake I will do it for you.'

I was trembling with anger as I stood waiting for his next move. He slammed the power handle shut and applied the brake. Without another word I climbed out and slammed the door shut. He gave her full power then. The 56's engine screamed defiantly and black smoke billowed into the air as the loco shot away. But at least I was off. A voice broke into my thoughts. It was Ian Farnfield, the driver who was waiting to relieve me.

'What's going on, Tony? I thought you wanted me to take it through for you.'

'I did,' I replied. 'But it appears that he don't.'

I followed Ian back into the lobby and thanked heaven that the stressful episode was over.

Or I thought it was.

At work next day I found myself booked on the same job with the same driver. It was impossible! According to the rules, any clash of personalities had to be reported to the supervisor; the parties would then be kept apart so as to maintain train safety. I never thought that I would have to invoke this clause, but I had no choice. The TCS sent me to our clerk and a yellowed form was produced from the back of a cupboard.

'Fill that in,' he said, 'and I'll tell the TCS to find another second man.'

I did just that and then went to sit in the mess room, which was full of train crews chatting and drinking tea. A job was found for me to second man a ferry set to Toton. Sitting down with a group of other second men I quietly told them my story.

'The old bugger must be going potty,' said one.

'He won't let it rest at that,' I said. 'He's too proud. He'll have to have the last word - you just watch.'

'Mind, he's just come in,' said another.

Sure enough the driver made straight for me.

'I've come to tell you, Tony,' he said in a voice loud enough for everyone to hear, 'that I've refused to have you on my engine. I've told them not to book us on together again.'

The words stung, but I wasn't going to let him have the last word.

'Oh, is that so? Well I've already refused to be booked on with you.'

For a few seconds the cabin was silent and everyone looked awkward. The driver scowled and walked out. Normality eventually returned. It was all very childish really, and it wasn't the way I liked to behave. But it wasn't my fault and I felt I had no choice but to stoop to his level.

30: The Branston Crash 1986

Our second exploding Class 20 'slow speed incident' occurred in 1986 as we were loading in Coalfields Farm. The guard was in the second man's seat reading the paper and I was just about to take a bite of my snap when we were interrupted by a loud bang and a shower of sparks. The guard was on the floor within seconds and the cab filled with smoke. I shut down the rogue engine, then we had to secure our train and go back to the shed light engine.

It was enough to make us suspicious - was this BR's new way of getting rid of surplus staff? It would probably be cheaper to blow us up than to pay us up!

On Monday August 4th 1986 a fellow passed man and myself began our very first week of road learning. The destination was Wellingborough. We sometimes rode on the 6V76 (Cliffe Hill - Hayes), other times we would go down in front of the HSTs. Whilst in Wellingborough yard we decided to look round the old shed buildings. Wellingborough loco (15B) closed in the mid-1980s. Some of the men retired, others went to Bedford. It was just a few years since we had both been in the mess room together. The doorway was blocked with a sheet of corrugated iron, but it was already half off and easy for us to push through. Inside the canteen, we stood amidst the old furniture and gazed around us in silence.

'It's like a time capsule,' said my companion.

On one table lay a dusty ASLEF journal; on the next was a chipped mug with dried tea stains inside. Such a deeply sad atmosphere! I couldn't help but think of all the happy railwaymen who'd sat there over the years, eating their grub, reading their papers, playing cards, laughing and joking - just as they still did in our own cabin.

The flapping of startled birds in the roof brought us back to the present and we quietly walked out, leaving the ghosts to their card games and cups of tea.

The following weekend brought one of many changes that were about to happen in my life. I left home and moved into a little house with my future wife. On October 10th I reached my hundredth driving turn and qualified for a higher rate of pay. Even so, I was still only a relief driver.

Much as I enjoyed being out on the main line, shed turns gave me a welcome chance to catch up on the gossip and have a laugh. Unless the men had formed a card school, that is - and then you couldn't get much out of them. When that happened I'd sink into my newspaper or go for a walk. One day all my favourite characters were in and we were having a right laugh. Unfortunately I had to bow out to get an engine ready, but I was so anxious not to miss the crack that I swept, started and prepped it in double-quick time. Racing back I was horrified to find no less than three card schools on the go! There'd be no more laughs from then on, just card talk and matches being moved up a peg-board.

In the end, to avoid being left out, I had little choice but to learn how to play myself.

58019, forty minutes after its collision at Branston with a steel train in 1986. Photo: John Tuffs

One Sunday, while second manning a cable-laying train at Swannington, I witnessed the ongoing bitterness between militant drivers and the guards who worked on coal trains during the miners' strike. We managed to take our train safely to Wigston – but what an afternoon the three of us endured! Even though I still have strong feelings on these subjects, I'm glad to think that I was not as extreme.

A month later I booked on the 05.35 to second man Frank Bailey on a Drakelow job. We'd been together all that week and as usual went light engine to Drakelow to pick up our empties. That week we'd been loading at both Cadley Hill and Rawdon and were destined for either A/B or C station. Once loaded we headed down the branch for A/B. The cab of 58019 smelled like a greasy spoon cafe as Frank cooked sausages and tomatoes.

Towards lunchtime we left the power station and ambled up the branch back to Coalville where we were relieved by Derek 'Mabs' Marlow. As the end of the week was approaching we decided to have a swift half in the Station Hotel in Burton. After a pleasant hour we parted company and I went home for a nap. Around 5 pm I was awoken by a thumping on the front door. Gathering myself together I looked through the bedroom window to see Andy Clarke, the Derby second man.

'Thank goodness it's not you,' he said when I'd got downstairs and opened the door. 'That's why I came round.'

I was till half asleep and couldn't think what on earth he was on about.

'One of your lads has come off the branch at Branston,' he explained. 'He's hit one of our steel trains. It's a right mess down there.'

His words brought me instantly to my senses.

'What was the engine number?' I asked as I set about making us both a hot drink.

'58019 - she hit the 31 that was hauling our train.'

'Oh no - Mabs Marlow! He relieved us at lunchtime. Is anybody... I mean do you know if anyone...?'

Andy quickly sensed what I couldn't get myself to ask.

'No, nobody's dead. They've all gone to hospital, all walking wounded I've heard.'

'Well, that's something.'

I knew the guard too - Brian Neal, or Chocolate Soldier as he was known due to his walking like one after a spell in the army!

When Andy left I sat down and tried to work out how it might have happened. It kept going round in my head until finally I had to go and look for myself. Accompanied by my wife-to-be I drove to Branston and onto the estate opposite the junction. Emergency vehicles of every kind stood in lines along the lane. Parking some way off we got out into the cold rain and walked towards the sodden field. Suddenly there she was - the engine I'd been driving only six hours earlier. Grasping my girlfriend's hand, I approached the fence. The sight was unbelievable! 58019 was on its side and covered from one end to the other in white foam. I could make out the underside of an HAA coal wagon and lots of other debris. What with the torrential rain, emergency lights and figures in HV vests the whole scene seemed quite eerie. Unsettled by it we decided to leave and walked slowly back to the car.

It was the big talking point in the cabin next day and the place buzzed with rumour and speculation. Both our men and the Derby driver had been released from hospital. It was said that Mabs had received a single yellow signal. Our job that Friday morning was to go light engine to Branston to fetch the thirty undamaged wagons and unload them at Drakelow. Again we found ourselves on 58024, an engine which seemed to have formed an unnatural link with 58019. We walked around the scene as 58019 was being righted. Signal sighting was taking place, with some drivers and an inspector riding up and down to check the signal which had temporarily been dismantled while a new relay box was put in place. We eventually left and unloaded the train. We picked up five more wagons to make it the usual 35-set, then by the time we got back we ended up on 12 hours.

Over the coming months there were three enquiries before it ended with Mabs being exonerated - but with a verbal warning to be careful in future! We will never know but even now, sixteen years later, he maintains that he received a single yellow signal.

A week later I was 07.00 ferry with the comical Barry 'Gassy' Gascoyne. A class 56 was standing at Bedford and needed to be brought back at Coalville. After a taxi to Leicester and a trip down 'on the cushions' we arrived to find 56071 on the depot. We prepared her and set off back to the Midlands with me in the driving seat. I was making good headway when we received a yellow for Kettering South.

'Typical signalmen!' I moaned. 'They would stop us now.'

But they weren't just stopping us - they put us into the sidings too. This made even the normally tolerant Gassy grumble.

'We'd better go and see what he wants.'

Putting on our orange HV vests we crossed the mainline to the big Kettering South box. 'Come in!' shouted a muffled voice as we reached the top of the steps. Wiping our feet we entered to be greeted by a small balding man, a typical 'bobby', with a woolly jumper, slippers and a duster over one shoulder. Everything in the box shone - the floor, the wood, and the glass of the block instruments.

'What's up bobby?' we asked.

'Sorry to stop you,' he said. 'The driver on the up express has reported a loud bang at Irchester and suspects it could be a fatality. Control wants you to conduct a line search in case there's a body.'

The very word gave me the creeps. Body! As the ruling stood, if a body is reported on or close to the track then the line is blocked. Our job was to either move it or mark it with ballast so the emergency services could locate and retrieve it later.

'Alright then, we'll search the line and carry on to Bedford again.'

'Thanks. If you go back to your engine and change ends, I'll pull off for you.'

With the signal off we whistled and acknowledged him. But I couldn't help feeling a bit sick inside at the thought of what we might find.

'Barry, what happens if we find one?'

'Well if it's dead we'll go through its pockets of course.'

He didn't mean it of course, but his jokey irreverence brought me back to earth. We carried on at caution but - thankfully! - there was nothing gruesome to be seen anywhere along the route.

'He probably hit a swan or something,' said Gassy.

On arrival at Bedford we reported that we'd found nothing, then carried on back to Leicester where Control informed us of a change of plan. We were to take our engine back to Beal Street and swap it for 56014 Tinsley's infamous run away loco. Once back at Coalville we filled in a report form. I was most relieved that we hadn't found anything of a gruesome nature.

56067 being lifted by the Toton breakdown crane at Branston in 1984. The loco had been manned by a Coalville crew. Just over two years later, another bad incident would happen in the same location. Photo: John Tuffs.

31: Big Changes

As 1986 went on I really got into the swing of branch work. I knew the branch from end to end, but on occasions our work took us further afield. One particular day I second-manned an 'Officers Special' which consisted of loco 31261 and a single officers saloon fitted with kitchen facilities. We took this small train and its complement of British Rail bigwigs from Burton station, stopping at various locations along the branch, before heading off for Derby via Leicester and Nottingham.

This was just one of many interesting jobs that came our way in the mid-1980s. A few weeks later we went to Hayes stone yard to bring back a train of PGA stone empties. Our engine was 58018 and we went light via Manton and Corby for that trip. My mate that night was the all-England man Phil Davies, a railwayman who signed everywhere.

The early part of 1987 proved to be run-of-the-mill work, moving coal mostly - which was what Coalville depot was all about. But our lives were destined to be anything but run-of-the-mill from now on. Big changes were afoot, and in the coming weeks and months we began to realise that life on the railway was changing for good. On Monday 19th January 1987 the grade of second man was eliminated. A driver would receive £2.50 for the loss of his mate. Luckily there were no redundancies and the second men would all be absorbed and eventually passed out as drivers. We were also beginning to lose our guards, though that was still at an early stage.

On Monday 13th April Craig Taylor became a registered driver - which meant that I now became Senior Relief Driver. From then on the driving turns came thick and fast. I still used my little driving turn symbol and would continue to do so until I also became a registered driver.

As most railwaymen and enthusiasts know, the 1960s brought the end of steam working in mainland Britain. And within a few short years many of the 'first generation' diesels that ousted the steam locos were also withdrawn and scrapped. Some classes didn't even survive the 1970s. Mass withdrawal of hydraulics was followed by the demise of many other familiar classes in the 1980s. While I enjoyed my life on the Leicester Line there was no ignoring the fact that our railways were being slowly run down. Many of the local collieries were being closed too - something that would have even more obvious effects for our depot.

On Friday 17th July I had to take 56010 to Leicester loco and leave it there while it underwent an exam. The TCS told me there was nothing to go back, but as our Coalville tripper had brought various wagons to Humberstone Road I could ride back with him. Humby Road (as we all called it) was full of withdrawn locos. Class 20s and 45s waited in various stages of dereliction. Among the lines of 25s, 26s and 27s stood 40060. A class 08 shunted wagons in the yard. After a while the shunting ceased and I recognised the driver as Dennis Simpson, our instructor from our traction trainee days.

'Hello, Tony,' he said. 'Long time no see. How are you keeping?'

I returned his greeting and we sat down to catch up on each other's gossip.

'What do you reckon to all these scrappers in the yard?' he asked. 'It's such a shame to see them all like this. There's nothing wrong with half of them!'

How true! Many had been withdrawn just because of minor faults or because they'd reached their maximum engine hours, shut down once they came in off a job, never to be started up again. In fact, although their paint was faded and they'd stood for about two years some still contained fuel. The sidings were being used as a temporary storage space for engines due to move down to Vic Berry's scrap business at Braunston Gate. They were tripped down by an 08 shunter on a daily working, the same trip bringing out the previous day's locos - now reduced to handy sized pieces!

'Let's go and have a look at them,' said Dennis. 'If you've got time.'

And so we took a walk amongst the silent hunks. Climbing up into one of the fusty-smelling cabs we found the controls covered in dust. Dennis dived into the engine room and put in the BIS. There was a 'ting!' and by the look of the fault lights it seemed that the loco's batteries were okay. He pressed the start button. The engine turned but refused to fire.

'I'll go and hang on the fuel rack,' said Dennis. 'When I shout, you press the button.'

From the darkness of the engine room I heard his call. The body rocked from side to side. Everything seemed all seized-up when all at once - boom! - the engine came to life and chugged unevenly. Dirty exhaust - a mixture of soot, spiders and dead leaves - billowed into the air and rolled around the yards. The compressors kicked in and began to build the main air. We shut her down and went to try the same thing on another, one that had stood a long time by the look of it. Again the body shook as Dennis hung on the fuel rack. The engine turned but it didn't look as promising as the first one. Then she started. There was a loud clanking but she wouldn't tick over properly.

'Shut it down!' shouted Dennis, 'Before she catches fire or blows up.'

Dennis disappeared again and I pressed the engine stop button. There was no response and it seemed as if the engine would shake itself to bits. I now used my T-key to push the button. Seconds later I heard a loud bang and smoke billowed out of the engine room. It filled the cab and drifted through the windows, attracting the notice of a shunter. A sooty-faced figure staggered out of the engine room.

'The bloody exhaust manifold blew!'

'Are you okay?'

'I think so,' said Dennis as he tried to clean off his face.

My T-key had done the trick. The engine was silent again, apart from the ticking of cooling metal.

''I think we'd better call it a day,' said Dennis.

He took out the BIS and we went for a cup of tea. The tripper arrived in the shape of a pair of Class 20s, a train of newly-repaired wagons from Marcrofts and a brake van. After a few shunts it was engine and brake back. The brake was leading over the branch, so I rode with the guard, standing chatting on the van's veranda. How wonderful it felt, as we looked out over the fields and trees and the warm sweet-smelling summer air wafted past our faces.

Then terror struck! As we passed through Bagworth the brakevan boards hit some raised ballast. I held on for dear life, expecting us to derail. The guard just laughed.

'I wish I had a pound for every time that's happened!'

Now I knew that we weren't about to hurtle down the embankment and end up in a pile of matchwood I just stood and watched the ballast fly in all directions.

'See, you don't realise what we guards have to put up with while you drivers are safely in your cabs!'

Lorraine, my future wife with Ivor Haskett at one of the Coalville Open Days in the 1980's

32: I Become A Registered Driver!

Posted on the second Wednesday of every month, the All Line Vacancy list was really a small book, which detailed driver and second man vacancies at depots all around the country. When September's came out, I was a bit shocked to see that Coalville had just one driver's vacancy, even though I'd half-expected it. But as long as no one registered an 8b or 14a move that job would be mine. I'd have to wait and see...

On Monday 28th September I booked on at 08.00 for the 6V76 to Wellingborough. It was a cold but sunny day. As I walked out in the cold sunshine to board my loco - 56061 - I found myself suddenly surrounded by the LDC. They were all smiles and handshakes. Anyone would think I'd won the pools! Well, for me, it was almost as good as. From the beginning of October I would be a registered driver. It took a while to sink in. In just eight years, I'd achieved my ambition. With that good news I climbed aboard my engine and left for Bardon. I felt touched: seldom do you experience people being genuinely happy for your achievements, but that really summed up the ambience of Coalville depot in 1987 - a community of decent railwaymen.

My letter of confirmation arrived on Monday 5th and I officially ended my driving turn symbol there and then.

The rest of the year was pretty routine, apart from the gales that hit the south and the West Country on the 16th October. At up to 105 mph they were the worst on record. So bad, in fact, that seventeen people were to lose their lives. My turn for that day - 6Z97 ex-Didcot - was cancelled for obvious reasons.

The following Sunday Mantle Lane railwaymen played a one-off football match against regulars from the Steam Packet pub. The final score was 2-2 and the afternoon was rounded off with a few beers.

At the very end of 1987 my father died after a long illness - a blow that seemed all the more devastating when it happened on my sister's birthday. Most people never come to terms with such losses, but my father was proud of having a train driver for a son and I knew that he would have wanted me to soldier on.

On the 13th January 1988 I road-refreshed Derby with ex-Burton driver Ray Bartram. He had to fetch 31282, which I drove back light - another chance for me to drive unfamiliar traction. Fresh opportunities also came on Monday 25th when I had 56015 in the new two-tone grey livery. Only one thing spoiled it. We were accompanied by the worst BR manager that any of us had ever worked under. He'd come along to examine certain safety issues that needed looking at. With an attitude that fell well short of human, it seemed as if he actually enjoyed being disliked! We took our train from Whitwick Sidings, loaded in Bagworth, then got relieved on the boards. We were also accompanied by two of the guards LDC. Their presence kept the gaffer on his toes - and thankfully off ours!

Though there were very few Class 45s left by this time, one or two still found their way onto the branch. On Wednesday 10th February I was 06.00 on shed. A new job - the York-

Bardons - had recently started and a variety of traction was booked on it. This gave our roster clerk quite a headache. Classes 47 or 20 were no problem - proper Coalville men and us younger chaps could work it. Sometimes, though, it was a Peak or a 37, so they'd have to find a driver (maybe an ex-Burton one) who knew the class. That day it turned out to be Eddie Brooks (ex Overseal and Burton). After swapping turns with another secondman, Karl Brailsford we then worked as far as Derby with 45140 (unofficially named Mercury). When Eddie asked me if I wanted to drive I leapt at the chance. So ended another era for me - it was the last Peak I ever drove.

On Tuesday 8th March I booked on duty for the 07.00 ferry. One loco needed fuel and water so I took 58025 on an uneventful round trip to Leicester. After disposing of the loco on the holding sidings I went to wash my hands, then headed for the messroom for a game of cards with the lads. The place was practically empty! Due to the increasing workload everyone was out earning revenue. A worried looking TCS, Ronnie Harrison, came over to me.

'Tony, I know you haven't had your PNB yet, but we've got a problem. Gord Sanders has dropped off the road in Drakelow. I've got no one else - will you go down with 58004 as a drawback engine and see the job out?'

Ronnie had looked after me on many occasions so even though it could end up as twelve hours I willingly agreed.

Arriving at Drakelow I positioned the engine at the back of the train's last wagon and waited. The Toton breakdown crane had just arrived and people from various departments were scurrying around the derailed wagons. After a while someone brought me a radio and coupled on. It turned out that the engine that had brought the crane had a broken leaf spring, so the Toton crew were instructed to commandeer my engine and I would take their 20009 back light engine.

As I walked down to it I could see that six wagons had come off and stood at unnatural angles. The trouble was due to the road spreading. And little wonder! Drakelow's arrival and departure lines had not been re-laid for years and instead of ballast the sleepers lay in spilled coal slack. The shunters cabin was full of people waiting to use the phone. In the corner sat Gordon, grinning and supping tea.

'You'll do anything for twelve hours,' I joked.

'You won't do so bad out of it either,' he replied, looking at his watch. '07.00 on this morning...'

Bidding him farewell I went off to relieve the Toton men on the Class 20. After swapping keys I set off, accompanied by Coalville guard Roy Butlin. By the time we got to Toton and returned by taxi we were on almost twelve hours!

33: Collision At Bardon

On Friday 13th May 1988, I had my first serious derailment. By now I was a regular on the York-Bardons, a job which continued for about 18 months. The start time was 06.00, but to save a taxi fare I would book on by the internal phone at the Moseley Street ground frame in Burton, then catch the 07.19 to Derby. Normally the train was standing waiting for us, the York men having secured it and then caught their train back home. The guard was usually waiting and ready to go.

This particular day we left as 7Z35, with engines 20086 and 20009 at the head of 25 empty stone wagons. Arriving at Cliffe Hill, we ran round the train by means of two ground frames. Once on the other end it was off down to Bardon. On the far side of the crossing the guard would drop off to set the points for an empty road, work the ground frame and call me in after I'd drawn the whole train across the points. I'd done it countless times over the previous nine years. The yard was always full of Tarmac tanks and it always looked as if you were about to hit the tanks - until at the last minute your wagons would slot in between them. It was only an optical illusion, but quite an unnerving one.

Summer was beginning early it seemed. The sun beat down on the countryside and a heat haze shimmered above the rails. I had changed into the other cab and could see the Derby guard working the frame in the distance. Then he waved his arm from side to side above his head. Taking it to mean, 'All's Well, Come Towards', I whistled an acknowledgement and began to propel the train into the sidings.

The usual illusion occurred - making it look like we were about to hit a train of tanks - only this time we actually did!

It seemed to happen in slow motion. What I saw turned my stomach. Two of the wagons shot into the air, lurched to the left and down the bank. The buffers clanged together along the length of the train and we stopped dead. I thought I would be shot through the cab window, but after hitting the glass I bounced back into my seat. A full can of hot water shot off the stove and showered the interior. Twenty-odd years of dust appeared from nowhere and billowed around the cab. Though uninjured, I was in shock. The only sound was the sound of the engines ticking over. For a few seconds I just sat looking at the gauges - then I snapped out of it. What about the guard? He'd been standing where one of the wagons had fallen - what if he'd been under them?

Leaping down from the cab I ran the length of the train and climbed up over one of the derailed wagons, praying that my weight wouldn't tip it further. To my relief I saw the guard standing amongst the debris. He was drawing hard on a cigarette as he stared at the mangled wreck of what was once the ground frame. He too was in shock.

'I realised what I'd done as soon as you started moving,' he said, 'but it was too late.'

He had failed to check what road the points lay for and had called me back straight into the tanks. With twenty five tanks standing there fully loaded and brakes on my empty wagons stood little chance!

We walked across to Bardon box to report it. The signalman made us a welcome drink while we awaited the arrival of the trouble-shooters. Before long the vans began to pull up and orange vests seemed to come from every direction.

'The breakdown crane is just leaving Toton,' the bobby informed us.

After a couple of hours it was decided that we work our 20s and the good portion of our train back to Coalville, where we had to make out reports. Three wagons had gone down the bank and two more were off the road. Over more tea we were interviewed by an inspector, who appeared satisfied with what we told him. He asked if I felt well enough to take both the engines and the guard back to Derby. I agreed and with my ticket signed I left light engine to Derby 4-shed.

The guard was blamed for not checking the points, but a Coalville guard also shared the charge. He had fetched in the tanks during the night, but after uncoupling and securing them he'd failed to set the points for an empty road, as was his duty.

56078 at Bardon Hill prior to leaving with 6V76 Stud Farm - Hayes & Harlington. Photo: Anthony Gregory.

By this time Humberstone Road was on its last legs, so we went to learn Derby St Mary's to trip wagons to and from Marcrofts the private wagon repair firm. I went on July 20th, reporting to the Derby TCS that I wanted a lift to the yard if possible. He told me that an engine - Peak 45103 - was going off shortly to fetch tanks from the Sinfin branch. We ran there light, picked up the train and put it into St Mary's. As the Derby driver shunted the tanks away I quickly made notes on the yard - how many dollies, etc - then it was light engine back to 4-shed. I dropped off the Peak at the station - the very last time I would be on a Class 45. They continued to be seen on expresses and indeed on the branch, until all of them (bar 45106 in green livery) were withdrawn on Thursday 4th July. 45106 didn't last long though - she caught fire at St Pancras shortly afterwards. Withdrawn 45s (97s) could be found on many depots, including Leicester. Many would end up in Vic Berry's yard where their power units were lifted out and, after being lifted off their bogies, they were cut in half to be added to the famous stack of Class 25s.

The railways as we had known them for so many years were being turned upside down by immense changes. On Tuesday 16th August a note went up stating that all drivers would receive a one-off payment of £200 for accepting the 'trainmen's concept.' This meant that secondmen or driver's assistants would no longer be required on trains or light engines. Driver Only Operation trials had begun in 1986 and were now being imposed. For the drivers it meant an extra £9.00. What better way to drive a wedge between the grades! Some greedy drivers welcomed the payment, even if it meant selling their mates down the river. Old hand guards who had worked with drivers for years now became hostile and would only speak to a driver if it was absolutely necessary to get the job done.

But the majority of drivers were saddened about the way that conscientious guards were being treated. Non-passenger DOO was introduced in stages, with the first trials running from Landor Street to Coalville. It then came in on Drakelows. A cabin was put up behind Moira signalbox and redundant guards were used as travelling shunters to load trains at Rawdon and Lounge. In 1988 the grade of guard at Coalville was finished forever. Some stayed on as travelling shunters, some transferred to other depots, while a few left the railways altogether. It was a sad end for a once proud body of men.

We drivers were now on our own...

The aftermath of the author's derailment at Bardon Hill. Photo: Tony Overton.

34: Vic Berry's and Other Stories

On Friday 9th September, along with a railway mate, I visited Vic Berry's scrapyard at Braunston to see if I could acquire a Class 45 power handle/reverser and a start lever. The place contained an amazing variety of classes. As well as their own shunter (03069) I counted classes 08, 20, 24, 25, 26, 27, 31, 40, 45, 47 and 50, as well as a few DMUs and EMUs. Most were for scrapping, though some had come for asbestos removal.

On Monday 14th November we saw the return of an 08 shunter to Coalville after an absence of four years. It was 08788 - nicknamed Henry The Wasp. Craig and I had already learned the 08s in October with instructor Dave Thomson. After swotting up the theory at Coalville, the practical stuff was done at Derby with 08511 and we were passed out on the 14th of the same month.

As another year came to close the changes to our depot continued. We'd already lost a lot of good men and were still losing them. The branch link men had long gone, three quarters of the ex-Burton men had retired, plus our guards of course. It was hard to keep track: they were there one week and gone the next. Ronnie Harrison, our popular TCS and one of the old school, finished on November 17th. But there were still enough of the old characters left for it to be recognised as the Coalville we knew.

Alongside my diary entries I kept a log of all locos driven. On my birthday, December 1st, I drove my last class 58 - 58042. Second from last, I'd had Toton's pet loco 58050. My last shift of 1988 was to take 08788 from Coalville to Burton MGR repair shops where our locos were stabled over the Christmas period. On New Year's Eve I spent some of the day with an ex-Derby mate who'd transferred to Birmingham New Street. With him at my side I drove 86245 to Preston and returned with 85035. The booked motive power was a Class 90, but it didn't show.

In January 1989, to mark our first ten years on the job, Craig and I received our 10-year ASLEF badge. Other than that it was business as usual.

On the 8th March I was 18.00 ferry. At 22.00 when Craig Taylor booked on we were told to take 56058 to Toton and bring back our 08788. As the Stenson branch was closed we had to go via Derby. Now, an 08 shunter is uncomfortable at the best of times and with a maximum speed of 15 mph going any distance on one is a killer! After a gruelling trip from Toton to Derby we were told that all lines were blocked by engineers possession at Sunnyhill - giving us no choice but to go all the way back to Leicester! That torturous trip finally ended at 07.00 the next morning, putting me on duty for 13 hours. We had aches everywhere!

Wednesday 6th June found me again on 07.00 ferry. Mabs Marlow and I went to Toton in a taxi to fetch 20094 and 20053. These engines had been part of a ferry set headed by 56064 that had set out for Toton the night before. Unfortunately they hit a car on the crossing at Castle Donington, killing the couple inside. This tragedy was brought home to us as we prepared the locos and were horrified to find bits of headlight and indicator glass on the bogies. One of the drivers involved in the smash refused to go across the Stenson branch ever again.

On Sunday 17th September all the men of the depot learned Stud Farm, a gigantic new stone quarry and railhead. Access was via Bagworth Junction opposite the old Ellistown Colliery. We went in two groups. the first went by minibuses on Sunday morning. Our group booked on at 13.00 to road learn the new yard. A few days later, heading back to Coalville from the Ashby direction, I was accompanied by one of the new young trainmen. As the evening began to draw in and the light began to fade we passed Black Bridge and accelerated up the straight just before Coleorton cutting. Then I spotted the two lights of a warning board for a temporary speed restriction. As I eased down the power handle the young trainman jumped out of his seat.

'Oh my God - twenties!'

It happened in a split second - the poor devil thought it was two Class 20s heading straight for us along the single line! I couldn't help laughing as the poor chap sat down again and tried to pretend that nothing had happened. Feeling a bit unfair, I reassured him by relating what happened to me when we had been on a return Didcot some years earlier. We'd been enjoying the last few moments of sunshine before it set in a watery grey sky when all of a sudden on the single line approaching Desford Pipes the driver zeroed the brakes. Horrified to see a Class 47 headcode approaching on our line, I jumped up and made for the door! But again it was just a warning board for a temporary speed restriction. It had only been put there that week and so we both fell for it.

Anyone can make mistakes, but in our job the consequences can be much more serious. As well it might have been for a gang of platelayers at Coton Park one day. Except that it wasn't really a mistake at all. For supposedly experienced railwaymen it can only be described as criminal carelessness that could have ended with a charge of manslaughter...

I had relieved a train at Moira for Willington Power Station. Passing through Gresley Tunnel I dropped towards the small coal stockyard at Coton Park and gave a warning whistle to a gang of platelayers. As they moved out of the way I was horrified to see that they'd been sorting out new sleepers on my line. Half a dozen lay across my path. I hit the emergency plunger in the cab and braced myself. With 35 wagonloads of coal behind me there was no hope of stopping. In my mind's eye I saw my engine derailing and crashing down the embankment onto the road below.

I'll give them their due: they quickly set about upending the sleepers from off the line and down the bank. But the closer I got, of course, the more reluctant they were to risk it. With just two sleepers to go the last two men upended one between them and sent it flying down the bank. The older - and wiser! - of them gave up. I was just feet away, but the younger man stayed on and with seconds to spare he managed to push the last one clear. Brave certainly - but lucky to escape with his life!

I came to a halt a hundred yards on and walked back towards them. I really turned the air blue before carrying on my way.

Later that same week I was discharging a train at Willington and had been stopped by the creep lights when a platelayers' bus drew up on the other side of the fence. They were such a common sight that I thought nothing of it until a voice attracted my attention. Opening my cab window I saw that it was the same gang.

'Sorry about the other day, mate,' said the head ganger. 'We'd have asked for possession, but it was only a short job and we thought we'd have it done before anything came along.'

'Have you reported it?' another one of the gang asked anxiously.

I told them again that it had been a bloody daft thing to do. But as no harm had come of it thanks to the two men have-a-go heroes I said I'd be letting the matter drop. I'd never been one to report everything willy-nilly. Hearing this the P-way men thanked me and went about their business.

Freight crews have to rough it far more often than passenger drivers. 'Passo' men often have clean and friendly mess rooms, with clean toilets, washbasins, soap and other luxuries. Freight crews can find themselves stuck in the middle of nowhere for anything up to twelve hours or have an exceptionally long run with next to no prospect of a break for hours on end. The call of nature can come at any time and it takes little imagination to guess what freight crews have to do when caught short. Isn't it lucky that Great Britain has so many hedgerows and fields! Guards were slightly luckier in their vans and, when they'd done their business, would often cast off a 'Guard's Parcel' from their veranda. Strong blue blotting paper was standard-issue to all such railwaymen.

On a sunny afternoon in 1989 I was joining the main line at Lichfield Trent Valley with loads for Rugeley Power Station. A class 47 stood at the signal on the up fast waiting to use the roads I'd just cleared. It was our Stanlow-Drakelow tank train. I knew who the driver would be, but he seemed to be missing from the cab. Up on the bank were two ladies absorbed in sketching the landscape. Looking back to the engine I caught sight of the driver - squatting down in front of the engine to relieve himself. Far from embarrassed, he stuck up a cheery thumb and carried on. As I recovered from the shock of seeing him I gesticulated towards the bank where the two ladies were already looking away in disgust. Seconds later I'd passed him by, so I never found out whether he saw them or not. But the poor girls surely never deserved to see such a sight on what should have been a pleasant day out in the country!

One evening in March 1988 my girlfriend and I took her mother for a meal at the Navigation Inn in Moira. After the meal we were joined by the rest of her family, but they wanted us all to go to Woodville working men's club. Being happy enough at the Navigation I decided to stay put. The only problem was, my girlfriend needed the car. But I insisted she took it, since I could get a taxi home or a lift on a Leicester Line train down into Burton. After they'd gone I got talking to a couple of former platelayers who I remembered working on the branch. A few pints and many railway tales later I nipped across to Moira west signalbox to phone Coalville to ask if anything was going down the branch. The next train down was the late running night Toton tripper but he wasn't yet ready to leave,

''I'll tell the driver to look out for you, Tony,' the signalman told me.

I went back to continue my chat with the ex-plate layers. Eleven o'clock struck but everyone was topping up and no one seemed in a hurry to go. Half an hour later, well past chucking-out time, I was getting anxious about my lift home. Everyone else was clamouring for another pint, so after token resistance the landlord put off most of the lights and began to re-fill pint pots. The revellers cheered and carried on - and I went up to the bar to have our own glasses refilled.

'I don't know, you'll lose me my licence,' the landlord grumbled, to no one in particular.

Ten minutes later a loud thump thump thump sounded at the side door. Everyone went quiet.

'Oh no,' groaned the landlord. 'I hope it's not who I think it is...'

He opened the door and a tall figure walked in. The first thing we saw was the dark uniform and silver buttons. The landlord looked sick with worry and everyone hurriedly pushed their pints away, as if trying to disown them. We awaited the reaction of the policeman.

'Is a Tony Gregory here?'

It was the guard off the night Toton that had stopped to pick me up. I supped the last of my beer and bade everyone goodnight. The landlord looked as if he was waking up from a nightmare. The guard and I went on our way, leaving some very puzzled yet relieved faces.

By the late 1980s the loss of our guards would be felt in more ways than one. The £9.00 a day 'reward' came at a heavy price, for it meant our shifts were long and lonely ones. Gone forever was the companionship of a train crew. There'd be no more communal mashings or fry-ups. Many chaps left their mash cans in their lockers and simply bought a can of pop instead.

The guard's place on Drakelow turns was taken over by a shunter who themselves were in short supply and were required to work twelve hour shifts. The 06.00 men, booked to finish at 18.00, would disappear at about 16.30 to get washed and changed and ready for the off. So by the time the next men booked on, had a cup of tea and made their way down to you it would be about 19.00. So two and a half hours would elapse before you could leave C-station. Most chaps would uncouple and run round themselves but if you were the wrong side a set of spring points would be in the way. These points are held in position by a strong spring - hence the name - so someone had to hold them over whilst you went through. Sometimes we would get the bunker men to do it for us but if they'd gone back into the complex you were snookered.

Unless you did it for yourself. I'd heard tales of a rail clamp hidden in the bushes for just that reason but had never seen it myself. A tale was told of a certain driver faced with just that problem. He put his bag on the holdover button of a 58, set the slow speed to half a mile an hour and took the straight air brake off. Jumping down the steps he held the points over whilst the driver-less engine trundled over them. Then he ran after it and jumped back in, thankful for not falling over.

35: Road-learning the Railway Mecca

On Monday 2nd October fellow driver Andy Haywood and myself began road-learning Crewe – known by many as Britain's railway Mecca. The 07.56 from Tamworth that we rode on most days offered a variety of traction: a class 86 or 90 more often than not, but with an occasional HST too. The express drivers were both pleasant and helpful with our route learning.

At Crewe some of our days were spent watching slide-shows in the road learning school; other days we would accompany an inspector around the vast railway yards as he showed us the many different moves and signal aspects we might expect to receive. Basford Hall Yard was losing its semaphores, so we found ourselves learning during a period of change.

Many road learners referred to Friday as POETS day, a cheeky acronym which stood for P*** Off Early Tomorrow's Saturday. And, as long as you'd made an effort during the week, our superiors didn't seem to mind too much. One Friday we had every intention of getting off a.s.a.p. As we ran into Crewe our plan was to dash up to the road learning school, get our ticket stamped, then get off home on the next express to Tamworth. Timing was crucial. Hurrying across the footbridge, we dashed down the platform towards the diesel depot. We had to cross the running lines so HV mini vests were essential. But Andy had forgotten his. That meant we'd have to share mine and make the crossing separately. Time was against us - but I had an idea. I quickly took the vest to him and told him to put it on. He did but looked puzzled. After a good look both ways to check that nothing was coming...

'Jump on my back,' I told him.

'What?'

'Come on, jump up, I'll give you a piggy back.'

He seemed a bit unsure but did as he was told. I wouldn't normally have entertained such an idea, but the line speed onto the depot was only 5 mph. We got our tickets stamped and repeated the exercise on the way back, catching our Tamworth train comfortably with time to spare.

One day, as we sat at the south end of Crewe station discussing moves round the station, a man walked by with a small dog on a lead. We didn't take that much notice - until the creature meowed! His dog was actually a cat. We'd never seen a sight like that before - and certainly not on a mainline station. When the odd pairing was far enough away we looked at each other and fell about laughing.

On certain nights we had to go on the actual job. My turn came on 7th November. I booked on at 18.53 and accompanied Ian Widdowson on the ex Bardon tanks bound for Ellesmere Port. Our engine that night was 58045. Leaving the empty tanks in Basford Hall, we ran light to the depot for fuel and water. We later headed back with a heavy train of loaded tanks. All was well until we reached Willersley dip where a combination of weight, gradient and the wet railhead defeated us. The 58s are renowned as bad slipping locos in wet conditions. We tried sanding the rails manually, then setting back and taking a run at it - but no amount of coaxing would move the train. So it was detonator protection time. Ian went back and I walked forward. The nearest phone to Moira West Signalbox was at Ashby Junction - quite a trek in the pitch black early hours. Imagination runs away with you at such times, especially when the silence is broken by the wings of a startled bird. Pheasants may look nice in daylight, but when they take off suddenly with their screech they're quite scary!

Assistance was organised in the shape of two Class 20s and I was told to remain at the signal to await their arrival. After forty minutes of spooky noises I heard the clickety-clack of their engines approaching down the single line. The familiar whistle of the 20s was quite comforting and as soon as he had shunted between the signals we went 'bang road' (wrong direction on the up line). We coupled them together but still could not move them. A Class 56 had to be sent for before we were able to move the stubborn tanks. We eventually pulled up at Coalville eleven hours after booking on.

They do say that things happen in threes. A week later we had finished at Crewe and had initialled our road card. I was unloading a train of coal in Drakelow A/B station with 56024. As I slowly passed the Daleks (hydraulic arms that closed the wagon doors after being emptied) all at once a jarring bang shook the engine. I stopped immediately and found that the arm had stuck out and ripped off both handrails. Whilst I waited an examination I was treated to a tour of A/B station by CEGB staff. But the run of bad luck didn't end there. Three days later I was on the same job and had got through alright - until the wheeltapper went back to examine the train.

'One to come out, Tony. Red card.'

The chargeman set up the road for the west departure as usual, hooked off the offending wagon, then sent me forward by radio. Once over the points the road was reset for the cripple sidings.

'Right-o, Tony,' said a voice over the radio, 'the road's set, give 'em a shove.'

I always enjoyed knocking cripples out at Drakelow. The shunter would hook off with a shunting pole and after a good shove back the wagon would roll into the cripple sidings and collide with the other wagons in there. Only on this occasion by mistake he left the rear portion foul.

'Oh no, they're foul!' cried a voice on the radio. 'Oh shit!'

He went off air. I stopped. The wagon derailed and the second report of the week was filled in.

36: First & Last Into Bagworth Bunker

1989 marked the centenary year for the Institute Of Mining Engineers, an anniversary which would be marked by the South Midlands Rail Tour. On Sunday 10th December they would be visiting locations along the Leicester Line, and so at 09.40 we took a taxi to Branston to await the rail tour. After a half hour delay a seven-car DMU turned up and we boarded it to conduct Saltley men across the branch. Our first stop was Rawdon Colliery, where we went through the bunker and stopped ten feet off the stop block. It was a move that seemed to displease the hard-core enthusiasts and they sent up one of the organisers to have a word with us.

'They've all paid good money,' he explained, 'so they want to complete the entire line.'

'We can't go any further - there's a stop block!'

'Yes, I know - but they just want you to touch the block with your buffers.'

We could hardly believe they could be so fanatical, but we shrugged and obliged the enthusiasts by literally taking it to the limit.

By-passing Lounge we made our way to Coalville. As we passed the depot all the enthusiasts rushed to one side of the DMU.

'It's a wonder we don't topple over with all that weight on one side,' I remarked to the Saltley men.

After Coalfields Farm we passed Bardon Hill and the now-closed Cliffe Hill Sidings. We went down the Stud Farm branch and into the now-closed Bagworth bunker sidings. The concrete bunker stood forlornly as it hadn't been used for a while and a locked spiked gate barred all entry. But British Coal had booked someone to let us through and once he'd unlocked the gates he climbed aboard the train with us.

'Enjoy it while you can,' he said. 'You're on the very last train to Bagworth bunker. They're going to demolish it any day now.'

His words made the hairs on the back of my neck stand up. I remembered something very important to me and couldn't help but tell the other train crew about it.

'Well, my claim to fame is that I was on the very first train to Bagworth bunker - and now I'm on the very last.'

As I spoke I became aware of an audience of eavesdroppers. They gave me a 'tell us more' glance, so I filled in the details for them.

'Yes, I was on the very first test train here in 1979. My mate was Derek Marlow and the guard was Cyril Blanchard. We were accompanied by a Derby inspector.'

The enthusiasts nodded approvingly at my tale. After touching the stopblock with the buffers we set back through the bunker. As the British Coal man climbed off to relock the gates

I was touched by sadness, remembering all the blokes I'd worked with at this location over the years.

Once behind the signal at Bagworth Junction we went full speed ahead down the single line to Knighton. Fog came down suddenly, blanketing the fields, and then they too were obscured as dusk turned to night. The job had been different to what I was used to and I'd thoroughly enjoyed both the novelty - and the nostalgia.

The Saltley guard had one of the new mobile phones, so we asked if we could call the Leicester TCS to book a taxi from Knighton. We got off there and said goodbye to everyone. Our taxi failed to turn up, so we ended up cadging a lift to Leicester station in an S & T van, before eventually getting another cab back to Coalville.

1990 was probably one of the most changeable years I've ever gone through. I got married, had my first trip abroad and welcomed our first child. The year also had some less pleasant surprises, though at that stage they could hardly be guessed at...

Like most Coalville men I felt settled, more than happy with my lot. We had our bad days, but they were always outnumbered by pleasant ones. At least we had the comfort of knowing that Coalville was a category A depot, which meant it was one of the least likely to close. What did we have to worry about?

On January 9th, working a Coalfields Farm - Drakelow C, I was stopped at DY126 signal in Derby. The signalman in the power box told me that the bobby in Moira West box had observed badly smoking bogies on engine 20108. By the time I'd got to Derby they were glowing red hot! Leicester fitters were called out to readjust the brakes, which had been badly adjusted previously so that they were binding.

On the 15th January - the 11th anniversary of my first day on the railways - I took off for Gran Canaria. The holiday would have been superb, had it not been for me nearly drowning on a jet ski and being attacked by an octopus. The constant hassle of timeshare salespeople hardly did much for the holiday feelgood factor either!

Saturday 24th February was my wedding day, when I was due to get hitched to Lorraine, my girlfriend of seven years. But things weren't going to plan. My lift to the registry office didn't materialise, so I had to walk. On my way to the Town Hall I came across ex-Burton driver Ray Large working on his car.

'Oh, look at you!' he exclaimed. 'You off to a wedding?'

'Yes - my own.'

'What do you reckon to this,' he said, pointing at his car. 'It keeps misfiring.'

'Er, is it the distributor? It could be cracked.'

I didn't really know what I was talking about, I was just anxious to fob him off and get going. The minutes were ticking by and zero hour approaching. But he wasn't going to let me go that easily.

'It can't be,' he said. 'It's not that old. Look at this wire, do you think that could be something to do with it?'

Against my better judgement I leaned under the bonnet. My best tie fell into the oil around his rocker box. I looked at my watch again: eight minutes to go!

'Look, I can't stop, Ray - I'm getting married in a few minutes.'

'Are you? Better get going then, hadn't you?'

I arrived at the Town Hall just on time and went straight in. As we were saying our vows some loud-mouthed individual came in to enquire about a future wedding. Just when I thought it couldn't get any worse Lorraine's dad's car packed up so we had to go to the reception by bus! Luckily we all managed to see the funny side of it and the rest of the day went smoothly.

The following week I was on an afternoon Rawdon-Drakelow. Booking on at 13.37 I went light engine to Rawdon on 56005 and loaded the train. Signalmen had now been ordered not to pull off for trains to leave a colliery until the booked time. Mine was 16.35, so by the time I'd finishing loading I still had an hour and a half to kill. Norman, the Moira signalman, apologised for keeping me, so I went off for a chat with the shunter in his cabin. We were interrupted by a knock on the door and opened it to find two chaps, one with a large and expensive camera, the other with some equally flashy sound equipment.

'Can you tell us what time that train will leave please?'

'I'd go now if I could,' I told them. 'But times are being monitored.'

They decided to wait, so we asked them to take a seat and mashed a pot of tea in preparation for a chat. Eventually the time arrived for me to get the engine started.

'Thanks for the tea,' the two men said. 'We'll go and pick a good spot to film you from.'

They headed for the old Swains Park sidings and I went to start the loco up. But the weather began to change and a huge black cloud drifted over us from the west. Surely they wouldn't bother now, I thought. As the signalman gave me the tip to leave the heavens opened and let loose a torrential downpour. Approached the entrance dolly I caught sight of the poor devils, totally drenched but still filming. Sometime later I came across a video depicting their efforts, so if you want to see a wet 56005 leaving Rawdon with both windscreen wipers on full belt the video is Railfreight 90, Vol 2.

A week later we began to conduct Toton men into Drakelow but had to first run around at Coalville due to both of Drakelow's east and west roads being relaid. It was a good week for me as I only lived a hundred yards from the Leicester Junction signal where we were booked to relieve them. Most of the Toton lads were fine but there were some not so nice ones who came out with lots of snide remarks.

'We could work this branch from Toton,' one said.

Perhaps they were right. No one could quite put their finger on it, but change hung uneasily in the air. Coalville didn't seem like the depot it had been just a short while before. Every week brought some unwelcome change to our familiar world. On Monday 19th March they pulled down the large goods shed and stores and on the same day the Bardon Hill tanks finished for good.

But there was one change that I welcomed! On Monday 26th my wife gave birth to our first child - James Anthony Gregory - and concerns for our future were temporarily forgotten.

On Sunday 8th April the whole depot went on a firefighting course at Toton. Half attended it in the morning, while I went in the afternoon lot. Inter-depot rivalry was always expected on such occasions, but some of Toton's younger element started goading us about our depot closing and how they would gain work from it. Not exactly tactful! A couple of our Coalville contingent took it very seriously and it almost turned nasty before both sides calmed themselves down.

Coalville's unique crossing box. Behind, on the site of the former 17c steam shed, is Marcroft's wagon and repair shops.
Photo: John Oldershaw.

37: Dark Clouds Gather...

On Friday 18th May I worked 6V76 from Stud Farm to Bedford, accompanied by two new trainmen. After completing our journey we caught a passenger train back to Leicester, then hopped in a taxi to Coalville. We walked into the cabin expecting the usual boisterous atmosphere - instead found a group of worried looking men.

'What's up with you lot?' I asked.

'There's rumours going about that the depot's shutting,' one of them said.

'Don't talk wet,' I said, but I quickly sensed by the mood of the other men that he might not be joking. 'There's a paper out there that says we're an A depot.'

'Maybe there is. But that don't mean anything. If they want to close us then they will do.'

My diary entry for that day was 'Heard that Coalville is down for closure. Could be just rumours, but it looks bad.'

My twelve years service wasn't that long compared to some, but even in that short time I'd experienced so much. I'd just turned seventeen when I started at Coalville - happy and impressionable - and pleased that the job entailed passing childhood haunts like Drakelow, Cadley Hill and Stapenhill. All that would be gone now, if the rumours turned out true. We all put on a brave face and tried to carry on as normal, but a gloom of uncertainty had descended over our once happy depot.

A week later Nigel Wilkins and myself took away Coalville's last shunter. 08623, an ex-Burton loco, was required at Burton MGR until it could be ferried to Toton. Standing at Leicester Junction for nearly an hour we chatted about our future. Although the rumours had yet to be confirmed Coalville's men were already making contingency plans. Nigel had opted to go to Nottingham, but I'd decided to do something different: instead of following the others to Toton, Leicester or Nottingham I was planning to go to Bescot for three years and then go on to Derby. I had distant memories of Bescot whilst bunking the shed alone on Bonfire Night 1973 and walking along those long lines of locos in the dark. My only other visit was in the early 1980s when we failed with an ex-Rugeley job at Walsall and were dragged to the depot for attention.

On Thursday 31st May I had worked a Willington job with 56008. After being relieved at Moira I was just about to order a taxi back to Coalville when the signalman told me I could get a lift off a train due on the up line. To my surprise the train was a cavalcade bound for Coalville open day. It consisted of 31507, D5054, Deltic D9016 and Hymek D7076 - all in green livery!

The open day was planned for Saturday 2nd June and as usual I had volunteered to work the weekend, Saturday to fetch the exhibits in and Sunday to man the engines, answer visitors' queries - and stop souvenir hunters. On the Saturday the trainman and myself made our way to Derby to fetch another cavalcade. Ours was made up of blue Generator D1500 (47401), the first Brush ever built at Loughborough in 1963, ex-class 46 97403 Ixion, Class 45 D100 and Class 25 D7672. This last one, now named Tamworth Castle, was in splendid ex-works condition and fitted with brightly-painted snowploughs. As the Derby trainman gave us the tip to set back off the vans (road) a steam special arrived in the station. The platforms were packed with enthusiasts. Some of them didn't know what to photograph first, but most gave priority to the steam loco before turning their cameras on us. A hundred flashes went off with what seemed like one accord. We stopped behind the signal then blasted away in the direction of Burton. Photographers crowded every bridge and embankment, raising their cameras to capture us from every angle.

Soon we got onto the branch and things began to calm down a little. Then we ran onto a 20-mph slack at Swadlincote Junction. With both windows down we chatted happily as the warm sun shone on the green fields. All at once we heard a loud scraping sound and looked back to see ballast flying in every direction. It looked like a mini meteor shower! Stopping to investigate we quickly found the cause: Tamworth Castle's snowploughs had hit raised ballast, scattering it everywhere and really spoiling the loco's ex-works appearance. Departing at caution we crept slowly clear of the obstruction and carried on to Coalville.

As soon as our engines were detached we went back light engine to Etches Park for a train of assorted coaching stock which we left on Goods Road 2. Back at Coalville our Class 47 was taken across to Mantle Lane sidings and disposed of.

Sunday saw another successful and well-attended open day. I arrived at 12.30 for a stint on the engines, then booked on duty at 16.57. By this time the crowds were thinning out and the stallholders were packing away their goods after another profitable day. We got together five of the former exhibits and prepared to take them back to Derby. Behind leading loco 47971 (ex-47480 Robin Hood) were 97403, D100, D5054 and D7076. The engines were left on the wall side at Derby loco and we rode back to Coalville on 47971. Thus ended another pleasant day, a tribute to all the organisers and volunteers who made it possible.

By this time Toton men had gained a foothold on our branch. Few signed it throughout, as yet, so on Thursday 21st June I had to take 56021 to Leicester and leave it for an A-exam. The second part of this job was to await Toton men and conduct them across the branch to Coalville, from where another conductor would take them to Drakelow. While I waited I sat in Beal Street cabin watching a world cup match. I've never been into football but watched it just because it was England playing. The night was inky black with torrential rain as I walked out to meet the Toton drivers with their Class 20s and loaded MGR train. The two old-hand drivers looked me up and down.

'Are y'all rate son?' they asked in their East Midlands accent.

We ran round at Knighton Junction and proceeded across the branch. Once the ice was broken we were chatting away like old friends. With the wet rails and the weight of the train I said that Desford Bank might cause us a problem. They said they'd heard it was heavy going across the branch. As we struggled onwards the weight of the train seemed to hang on to us all the more. We slowed for the 15-mph junction at Desford and never regained any kind of speed after that. After slipping badly we experienced fluctuating amps and the locos began to overload. We had just got out of the dip at Bagworth when the engines gave up the ghost and no amount of coaxing would get them any further. Time to get assistance from Coalville! I used the signalpost telephone at Bagworth to contact Bardon Hill box. After a long and soaking wait at the detonator protection help finally arrived in the shape of another Class 56, which only just got us moving enough to get restarted.

Wednesday July 4th - American Independence Day - also marked the cup final between England and West Germany. I arrived at work at 18.00 for the ferry. I'd told the TCS not to find me a job, as I wanted the chance to cheer for my country. The atmosphere in the cabin was tense and exciting, but just before the game started our TCS came in.

'Sorry, Tony, but there's a couple of engines to take to Leicester for fuel and water.'

The author's derailment/collision with 47195 and 56025 in 1990.
Photo: Tony Overton.

We grumbled a bit, but it was our job and so we set off with 56025 and Stanlow Tanks engine 47195. We managed to watch some of the match there, but just after half time the fitter's mate came in and told us the engines were ready to go back. I asked the other driver if he wanted to try and get back to the depot in time for the second half. He agreed. We left Beal Street and ran to Knighton. Changing ends we hurried down the Leicester line, changed ends over the dolly at Coalville, then proceeded onto the shedside as instructed. The three throw points lay for the dock, so my conscientious mate got off, changed them, checked them each with a brake stick and called me on.

As we negotiated the points and headed onto shedside our world suddenly turned upside down. Bang! Bang! Bang! The 56 seemed to bounce along the sleepers like a giant metal kangaroo. A sickly scraping of metal followed by a huge bang that seemed to propel us further forward. The only thing I recall in those few seconds was zeroing the proportional brake and glancing across to my mate as he tried to remain on his feet. Then suddenly silence reigned. Brown summer dust circulated the scene and the smell of creosote from the broken sleepers filled the cab. I shook my head in an attempt to clear it. A group of men came running from the office. We opened the cab door and went to climb down the bogie steps - but they weren't there! The bogie was crosswise across the tracks, so I had to jump down onto the dusty ballast.

'Are you alright lads?' the men asked when they reached us.

I looked at one of them and as my legs buckled due to the shock I asked them who had won the football match. They looked at me gone out.

'Who won?' I repeated.

'West Germany,' came the reply.

Dismayed I set about assessing the damage. It seemed as if our 56 had smoothly continued down shedside when for some reason the points altered and the heavy 47 had gone down the shed road, pulling the 56 off. Then the cabs crunched. As you stood in the 47 you could practically look down onto the 56. We were taken to the cabin and given sweet tea to ease the shock. Our TCS spoke to us gently. After asking us if we were okay he said that amongst the many other unexpected guests we were to receive that night was inspector Don Tennant from Toton, whose pager had gone off while he and his wife were dining out. He looked sympathetic but his wife was far from impressed! After submitting a verbal and a written report we were told to go home - but not before photographs had been taken at the scene.

We heard nothing else and it was decided not to put the dock and the shedroad back. They would have to cut off the coupling to part the engines and 56025 stood there for a week before leaving for attention.

38: Countdown To The End

On 17th July, after booking on for the 14.35 local tripper, I was invited into the conference room for a so-called counselling session. Intended to guide us through our redundancy notices and answer our queries, it was something we'd all have to go through in the coming weeks. I was introduced to some of the LDC (local district council-union), a sectional council rep, a personnel officer and a couple of smug managerial types. I tried to look unconcerned as they went through all the formal bulls**t., but I knew this was it.

After half an hour I left the room, bewildered and washed-out. I now knew for sure: Coalville depot would close on October 1st 1990 and there was nothing we could do about it. Our A-depot status was apparently a clerical error - we were actually a C-depot and we might as well have been a Z-depot for all the good it would do us.

'Well, what happened?' people asked as I walked into the messroom. 'What did they say to you?'

I repeated everything that had been said to me, but I saved the best till last:

'They've fetched me off my job tomorrow to go on a depot visit.'

'What - where to?'

'Bescot.'

'You're joking!'

Leaving behind a cabin full of worried faces, I picked up my bag and lamp and got into the taxi that was waiting to take me to Lounge opencast colliery.

Bescot made Coalville look like a garden railway. I couldn't believe how vast and busy it was. After locating the LDC office, I was introduced to some of the staff. They seemed friendly enough, and after making me a cuppa they took me on an exhausting tour around their depot. It didn't seem a bad place, but I was happy at Coalville. At the end of it I found a lift home with a Bescot man on 56070. It had been a long and eventful day and I couldn't help nodding off in the cab.

Next day I was back in the swing of things. I put my worries at the back of my mind and tried to act as if nothing had happened. The days and weeks - and eventually the whole summer - seemed to pass by rapidly. Coalville's men put on a brave face but they couldn't ignore the black cloud that seemed to hang over our place. Our once happy depot had gone forever.

On August 3rd I made visits to the depots at Derby and Saltley. By the first week of August the Toton men began to come up the branch. Some had already signed the branch, while others needed conductors. Most of them were decent chaps and told us how much they regretted our closure. But there were one or two who positively gloated at the prospect of new work at our expense.

Over the years a group of us - drivers and guards - had regularly used a free pass and gone off together for a day's sightseeing and a few beers. Our latest, on the 18th August, was to Lincoln. With the sunshine beating down on us we scaled the steep streets of the market town. We found a nice pub and sat there chatting over a few beers the closure was hardly mentioned at all. No one wanted to spoil the day.

The countdown to October 1st had begun. The leg-pulling and horseplay still went on but a genuine camaraderie existed. When the All-Line Vacancy list arrived on the Wednesday we saw that the five Bescot vacancies had been cancelled so it looked like I would be going to Saltley, my second choice.

For the next month I was booked onto various Willington jobs. We were alright to go there as normal, but due to a missing diamond crossing at Stenson Junction (a new one was being built in Germany) I had to run round on the new bank at Toton.

The clock kept ticking by. Then, on the 10th September, came the closure of the long-established P-way offices at the back of the goods shed. Although they were nothing to do with us, as such, we knew all the platelayers and their gaffers. It was one more nail in the coffin.

My last working week at Coalville began on Monday 17th September. It was a gloomy week and it often seemed like I was the only train on the branch. On Monday I went light engine to Lounge with Brian Neal. After loading the train, I was relieved at Moira by old-hand Coalville driver Albert Pickering. He didn't seem his usual self - but which of us was just then? Tuesday was pretty much the same, but this time it was ex-guard Geoff Wardle who looked down in the mouth. On the Wednesday I had to endure a working to Lounge with Toton men on two Class 20s before relieving my train with 56019. Talk about rubbing salt into a wound!

With just two weeks to depot closure, a not-so-happy bunch of Coalville men. Photo: Nigel Walker.

Friday I remember most clearly though. I rode up with Frank Bailey but felt like s**t. The blackest day loomed ever nearer and I couldn't rid myself of the sick anxiety in my stomach. The working life I'd settled into was about to change forever. I thought of all the people who'd gone through the same thing: the mining communities who'd had their pits closed, the miners who had given their best years only to lose their jobs, friends and security, facing a grim choice between early retirement or a new job in strange surroundings. At least I'd be able to continue on the railways.

I relieved a driver on 20094 and 20053 and loaded the train again with Brian Neal. Albert Pickering relieved us at Moira and I then rode down to Burton with him. We never passed another train on the way down

'Just think how it used to be...' I remarked. 'There'd be trains waiting at virtually every peg.'

After a warm handshake I dropped off at Leicester Junction. To mark the occasion - or rather to drown my sorrows - I went for a pint in the Black Horse in Moor Street.

My diary entry for Monday 24th September reads: 19.00 spare, no work, done at 22.00.

By now the skip in the shed yard was full of papers, forms and traction bulletins emptied from the office cupboards.

On Tuesday I was 18.00 ferry. It turned out I needn't have shook hands with Albert on Friday as he was acting rider with me, taking 56019, 56010 and 56026 to Leicester for fuel and water, finishing at 21.30. Why not? There was nothing else to do.

Wednesday arrived and again I was on the ferry. Our pool table had gone, leaving just four circles pressed into the lino, a poignant reminder of all the fun and light-hearted sporting rivalries played around it. I took 56078 to Leicester and rode back on our additional ferry, consisting of 56019, 47190 and 58040. Done at 21.45.

The next night I was handed a small brown envelope containing £42.10. We all got the same. The depot's Welfare Fund had been officially wound up that day and that was our share-out. After taking 56019 for fuel and water, I was done by 20.30.

Friday finally came, our last official day as a railway depot. I donned my uniform with mixed feelings and, for once, decided to wear a tie as a mark of respect. Driving through the gate I was overcome by a really weird feeling: the shed was full of 56ers and looked just like it had on my first morning back in 1979. If it wasn't for the locos' drab grey livery it might have been that day all over again... And this time the yard was dotted with camera-toting railway enthusiasts who'd come to mark the occasion and say their farewells.

18.00 ferry again. I sat in the office with some of the lads, watching the engines leave the shed for Leicester and Toton. Finally there were just three left. The TCS swivelled round in his chair and looked straight at me.

'Well Tony, you have the honour, you're the last Coalville man to take engines off shed. These three are for Toton and you're back passenger. Oh, and John Healey is going with you.'

I turned to face a forlorn-looking bunch of blokes and said jokingly:

'Did you hear that - I'm the last Coalville man to leave with a train.'

'Oh no,' said the TCS. 'I said you're the last driver taking the last engines away. There's still a train to go yet.'

'Who's on that then?' I asked.

'The honour's for Albert Pickering. He'll be the last to leave, with a Coalfields - Drakelow.'

'Oh well, it's still not bad,' I said. 'The last engines, it must mean something.'

John Healey turned up just as I was leaving the office to prepare the engines.

'Anything doing Tony?'

'Yes - we're taking the last engines to Toton.'

I made ready 56026, 56019 and 58040. As we left the shed the small crowd of enthusiasts set up their cameras to record the scene. On the down line fifty detonators had been laid for Albert to explode. It was a sight I'd dearly have loved to see.

We arrived on the fuel line at Toton and walked across to the booking-on point.

'Coalville men just bought three on,' I announced.

'Ex-Coalville men don't you mean?' said the TCS.

His cruel tease didn't go down very well with us at all. Seeing our faces he quickly tried to make amends.

'Sorry lads, but all good things must come to an end, as they say.'

Our lift back to Leicester was on 31503 Sister Dora, ironically a Bescot engine. The Leicester crew were a bit more sympathetic. A taxi took us back to Coalville. By the time we got back the messroom was empty, just the TCS and a couple of blokes chatting. A red-eyed driver took down the final week's rosters and carefully rolled them up, intending to take them home for a souvenir. Albert had exploded his fifty detonators, a grand finale captured in scores of photographs.

'Everyone's up at the Red House,' the TCS told us. 'Are you going?'

'Wouldn't miss it for the world,' I said.

The pub was packed with railwaymen. Not just those from this last shift but many of the day men who had gone home and got changed before coming back to the 'happy party.' Should we be acting like this? I wondered. Shouldn't we all be sitting round looking glum? But the blokes didn't want that - they just wanted to enjoy themselves. And deep down so did I.

There was still a big farewell do planned for the following night - during which many pints would be sunk and just as many tales told.

I finished my diary entry for that day with the words 'The End'.

That put paid to half the depot's complement. Drivers and trainmen who had opted to remain with East Midlands Freight would be reporting to Leicester and Toton depots on October 1st. Along with others I'd still be booking on at Coalville as normal, but without engines we were hardly likely to be doing much! Six men opted for retirement, while the remaining drivers and train men - now classed as redundant - would go on the All-Line Vacancy list and eventually get a move to either Derby, Saltley, Nottingham, Bescot or Shirebrook.

The Saturday night do came and went with mixed emotions, but our final day at work was yet to come - on the 12th October.

On Monday I was 08.00 on, not 08.00 shed or 08.00 ferry, just 08.00. They hadn't even the decency to book us off. Confirmation came through that I had a vacancy at Bescot. As the week went on we had to hand in our Bardic lamps and manuals.

Our trains were now being worked by Toton men, who would glance sheepishly across at the depot as they passed. On one occasion my mate Craig Taylor - now a Toton man - came up and I nipped across the boards for a chat. The situation got increasingly bizarre. Coalfields Farm was playing up and waiting for coal. The Toton drivers began to bail out and go home by taxis - but they wouldn't allow any of us to work the trains. Our TCS was besieged by drivers demanding their PNB. Again he phoned Toton to suggest that some of the jobs be manned by Coalville men. But they wanted to make their point.

'No Coalville men will take any of our trains whatsoever.'

That's what we felt like now - outcasts. But if they were to rob us of our dignity, at least they decided to let the retiring drivers leave at the end of the first week instead of having to kick their heels for the whole fortnight.

And so we killed time by wandering around the town. We washed cars, played cricket, anything to pass the deadly hours. On a couple of days we all chipped in and cooked ourselves a great fry-up. For a while at least the old happy spirit returned to us.

Thursday was the last time I would share a depot with ex-Burton men. They would be finishing the next day. But we had one or two scores to settle first. Gordon Sanders and his enamel mug for a start. Gord had a habit of swilling out his mug after a drink and always splashed the dregs of water over anyone who was in his way, especially if you'd been pulling his leg. He must have wet a thousand faces over the years. So while he was out of the cabin Tony Parker and I put the precious mug under a loaded ballast train that was being examined on Goods 2. The train began to move and with a loud crunch flattened the mug. Giggling like a couple of kids we watched as splinters of enamel flew everywhere. When the train had gone we picked up the flat piece of metal and solemnly presented it to him.

So ended our first week. But we had another week to go.

The last week I was 15.30. We had nothing to do but tinker with our cars, play cards - if you could find anyone to play with - or else we nipped up to Mantle Lane signalbox to talk to the bobby. Only 3 - 4 hours were spent actually working, the rest of the time we just tried to quell the boredom.

The last day arrived, a relatively warm and sunny one for mid-October. Again I wore a tie as a mark of respect. Cameras were clicking all over the place. Some men stood talking while others tidied up. A crowd of us walked up to the chip shop via Goods 2 and nearly got run down by the Bescot ballast train.

'There's your new mates, Tony,' someone said.

It didn't go down very well, especially on this night. Back at the depot more photos were taken against the background of an engine-less shed. Only wagons filled the holding sidings. Men began to shake hands and walk away through the gates. We had our photos taken against the nameboard of the Mantle Lane signalbox and outside the gate below the depot sign.

At 19.00 a loud and angry Mick Geary had the honour of being the very last driver to book on at the depot. We had the very last farewell do up at the pub and this time it really was the end. After nearly thirteen years it was farewell to life on the Leicester line - as a Coalville driver anyway. I still worked the branch from Bescot for three years, then after eight years away I re-learned it in 2000 whilst at Toton depot.

THE END

The author alongside a poster announcing the open day of 1990. By the time of the next - and last - one, the depot would be closed. Photo: Dennis Wright.

Postscript

Just After

So Coalville depot No 2 (or Mantle Lane) was gone for good. The prefabricated BR building stood locked cold and empty. Even now, 13 years later, I often wonder what the signalmen who manned Mantle Lane box thought after we'd all gone. They were still kept busy but not with engines coming on and off shed but to accept and offer Bescot - Bardons.

I still came up the branch and even went onto our old holding sidings more than once to get water for a class 31. Alien classes were now a routine part of my job; no longer was it a thrill to have a class 37 or the new class 60. We would wait ages to enter Stud Farm as there was always another train in front of us loading. Many Bescot men would secure and leave their train on the neck at Bagworth Junction - the exact spot where all those years ago Cyril Kendrick and I almost ran into a gang of platelayers. So the situation entailed a lot of light engine running to and from Bescot as crews bailed out due to bad time. I would arrange to go onto the shed just to enter our old depot building and offices shorn now of all but basic equipment and anything technological had long gone. As I sat sipping tea and chatting cheerily to the ex-guards the Bescot trainmen eyed us sympathetically. Their depot had never closed. The older Bescot guards knew what we must have been feeling, but the younger newer ones must have wondered what all the fuss was about. Whenever I passed by the old shed I would stare hard at the windows, remembering all the things that had taken place on the other side: the rush of us young chaps hassling our roster clerk on a Thursday afternoon for Friday off to go to our night clubs; the smoking fax machine in the office; my two days of torture whilst passing out on MP12.

Though Coalville depot was gone, daily life on the railways didn't change that much for me. I was to have another serious collision (Between 47340 and E85103 the latter being withdrawn) and a class 58 (58001) very nearly on its side with 3 wagons off, in Drakelow about a mile and half as the crow flies from Mabs' 58019 do. But neither incident was my fault. Another time, just seconds after my companion Bescot driver asked if I'd ever had a derailment, we dropped off the rails in Bescot with the Tyseley breakdown crane. But that was due to the state of the rails.

With my mutual exchange to Saltley and three years with RFD I was to suffer many incidents and blow-ups. Not with Class 20 slow speed modules but with time-expired Class 47s which blew up and failed themselves. By the mid 90s these ageing machines should have been on leisurely trip working down some short branch instead of being thrashed to bits on freightliners. With a full digger on to Wembley, Eastleigh, Crewe, and all the rest of the destinations of this country we visited, I endured more failures during this period than any other time, with so many incidents that it would require another book to log it all.

Presentation of nameplate to Snibstone Discovery Park by ex-Coalville men at the 1993 reunion. Photo: Anthony Gregory.

Present day.

After an enjoyable 7 years at Saltley I reluctantly left to go to Toton, a depot that had been a favourite from my spotting days of the early 1970s. Toton will always mean a lot to me for that reason. Though there is still a good percentage of ex-Coalville men at Toton, I had now joined the ranks of the very men who took our work before and after we closed. None of it was their fault, though, and it was, and still is, a fine depot manned by a good bunch of blokes. With all the present-day red tape none of the tales in Life on the Leicester Line would be allowed to take place on this modern railway of ours. They'd be a serious embarrassment to it. Still, even though we are all older now and the job is slightly more mundane but I still record the day to day events in my diary.

The depot today.

Now and again, after visiting old mates or taking the family shopping, I have spent a couple of minutes looking over the locked gates (just to have a look at the dereliction process that the years bring as they pass by). Only roads Nos. 1 and 2 are left. A red HBA wagon has stood forlornly on number 1 road for many years. The only other wagon, long forgotten by TOPS, is an ordinary HAA coal hopper on the stop blocks on the longside roads of Mantle Lane. Over the years many young saplings have grown up around it and obscured it from view.

In April 2002 I phoned the signalman at Mantle Lane box and asked ask him to describe the scene today. Regular branch signalman Keith Waters told me that the old depot building has recently been boarded up and is due to be demolished, along with the old brick building near the box. Mantle Lane box has been re-painted in Midland colours, but alas has a nameboard but no letters. A rail grinder stands on No 2 road ready to depart to work on the branch. The branch is still used from Burton end for access to Drakelow C, Hicks Lodge and Swains Park, and from Knighton direction for Bardon and Stud Farm.

The future.

Lounge sidings are used by Toton crews to run round trains of empties for Hicks Lodge, but it is down for closure as a distribution park is rumoured to be built on the site. There is also a glimmer of hope that the branch will one day re-open to passenger trains and stations built, especially at the site of the new Conkers Discovery Centre built on the site of the former Rawdon Colliery but we'll have to wait and see.

As for me, in May 2002, I opted out of the freight side after 23 years. Having most recently worked for private freight company EWS (English, Welsh & Scottish Railways), I am now employed by Midland Mainline at Derby and enjoying a very different kind of traindriving.

Coalville Depot Open Days

In 1977 my chief, Mr A.B. Wise, Area Manager at Derby, sent a letter to his assistants stating that the Derby St Christopher's Railway Childrens Home needed to raise a large amount of money to pay off the costs of a new building which had just been opened by HM The Queen Mother. Ideas or suggestions should be sent to him for consideration. After some thought I came to the conclusion that an Open Day at Coalville Depot would attract lots of interest, not only from the staff and the people of Coalville but from hundreds or even thousands of railway enthusiasts. I got in touch with Mr Wise and set out my ideas.

A few weeks later Mr Wise informed me that he was very interested in the idea and he would be seeking higher authority for this to take place. This was in August of that year so any approval given would be too late for an open day in 1977 but Mr Wise was hopeful that one could be arranged for 1978. He also asked me not to say anything until he was sure that the go-ahead had been given. In April 1978 I was invited to attend a meeting in Derby to discuss a "proposed Open Day". This meeting came as a surprise as I had heard nothing for months and I had thought that the idea had been quietly shelved.

The meeting, chaired by Mr Wise and including representation from the Divisional Managers Office at Nottingham, was very positive. Mr Wise opened by saying that the proposed Open Day had been agreed and our meeting was to discuss the organisation necessary to make it a success. A Sunday in August would be the ideal time and I was remitted to form a Committee to move the scheme forward.

As I left the meeting it struck me that I had a lot of work to do. Coalville Depot was to hold a major Open Day in about 16 weeks and I had no experience, just my ideas and a promise of support in high places. And of course wonderful staff who I knew would be very enthusiastic about this once I'd told them the news.

My first job was to form a committee. It so happened that on the day after the Derby meeting I was the management representative on a Health and Safety Walkout with local drivers and guards' representatives. The day was spent at locations along the line between Knighton South Junction and Burton, including the various collieries and Drakelow power station. During our lunch break I discussed this proposal with them, the men being Coalville drivers Jack Knight and Jim Robinson and Coalville Guard Cyril Blanchard. Their response was immediate and very supportive. It was agreed that to get things moving Jim Robinson and Cyril Blanchard represent the drivers and guards respectively on the committee.

I then turned my attention to forming the remainder of the committee. Discussing the proposals with supervisory and clerical staff I again received massive support and was able to co-opt Mike Evans and Ian Briggs.

The first meeting was held, and it was obvious that the idea had really developed, more ideas were forthcoming, a list of exhibits was drawn up, the open day was very firmly "on"

Subsequent meetings looked at Open Day Organisation, Safety of the Public, Refreshments, Advertising, Police, Admission charge, Programmes, Public Address System and a thousand and one other points which cropped up and were dealt with by the committee.

Mr Wise told me that we could have a Diesel Multiple Unit, apparently we couldn't have a passenger train service but we would be allowed to operate a short shuttle service along the line called "Down Goods 2 line".

Conducted by Charlie Farren, Cadley Hill No. 1 returns to Snibston after visiting the 1996 Coalville Open Day. Photo: John Tuffs.

Staff interest intensified and when we asked for volunteers to attend as stewards or in any capacity, many put themselves forward. Mike Evans arranged a large number of trade stands and carefully measured and allocated space for all traders. Ian Briggs was the first treasurer and dealt with the collection, accountancy and payment of all bills. Jim Robinson arranged and manned the first aid point, while Cyril Blanchard assisted in the control and distribution of stewards.

Many non-committee members were heavily involved, Doug Elliott was everywhere doing everything and anything, Ron Harrison and Steve Peters juggling train crew rosters to arrange collection of and return of exhibits, and also allocating stewards to sit on exhibition locomotives during the open day. Most of the depot staff and some of their wives helped out in a variety of ways to make the day a success. All were volunteers with no payment for the considerable work that they did.

As far as exhibits were concerned, Coalville normally had freight classes 08,20,47 and 56 there every weekend, so their presence was no problem. To make the line-up more attractive the committee drew up a list of locos that would enhance the show. I said that I would try to obtain a varied selection. Some were easy to obtain, with a lot of co-operation from the

Divisional Control office at Nottingham, classes 25 and 45 were obtained from Toton, a suggestion from Mike Evans and Steve Peters that the class 31 on the Doncaster to Cliffe Hill on the Friday before the open day be swapped with a locally-based class 47 which would work the return Cliffe Hill to Doncaster .The locomotives then working the Monday services and swapping again at Coalville to return the class 31 to Doncaster was agreed, hence the open day now had a class 31.

Two Thornaby-based class 37/5s arrived at Toton on Saturday morning on the Lackenby to Corby train and were due to spend the weekend at Toton before returning north on the Monday. Agreement was quickly given for these locomotives to appear at the open day where they attracted a lot of interest.

The first open day produced 37501 and 37502 (This was in blue livery)

On the Friday before the open day the control advised me that one of the last class 24s (24081) was at Toton but was to work back to its depot at Stoke that same day where it was needed for weekend ballast duty. I had a quick word with Mr John Gradon the Trains Officer at Nottingham Division and after he contacted Stoke it was agreed that 24081 could attend the open day while a class 25 was sent from Toton to cover the ballast workings. This was a very welcome and unexpected guest.

Toton were also happy to provide a class 44 (44008)

I had also been trying to obtain a steam locomotive. Ex-LMS Crab 2-6-0 no 2700 was being repainted in Derby Works and I eventually received permission to bring it to the open day. Even though it was not in steam it proved a very popular exhibit. Cadley Hill - one of the collieries on the Coalville line - was still using steam locos for shunting and through the good offices of Mr Chris Boyle of the NCB I obtained one for the open day, this time in steam.
In 1978 some of the early diesel locomotives were in preservation on various sites. Butterley had some and I was able to arrange for a class 44(D4) to be present.

All in all the exhibits on show were of a high quality and all were cleaned by the Coalville staff on the Saturday morning to make them presentable to the general public.

Another interesting exhibit was a large independent snowplough, normally kept at Leicester Depot. It was duly collected on the Friday. Unfortunately it did not like Coalville Yard. As it was being propelled into the yard it became derailed and for a time prevented any movements on or off the depot. It eventually was carefully stabled but we did not request it again!

Another unexpected exhibit was the official British Railways cinema coach which showed a series of British Transport Films throughout the day.

Finally the big day arrived and our planning and arrangements were tested to the full. As we had never done anything like it before there were some rough edges and areas that needed improvement but overall we had over 3000 visitors, many letters of congratulation and a good press.

From admission charges of 20 pence and from the traders' donations and charges we were able to present a cheque of £1300 to St Christopher's much to their amazement and satisfaction.

A meeting was held to discuss the open day, lessons to be learnt and the way forward. Was the event to be a "one off" or was it to be repeated? We agreed to hold another open day in 1979, take on board the lessons learned, but generally keep to the successful plan of the 1978 event.

The 1979 event again proved successful, the variety of exhibits based on the 1978 formula of three types again proved to be a very big crowd-puller. The three different types of exhibits were. 1) as wide a variety of different British railway diesels; 2) as wide a variety of preserved diesel locos; 3) the working steam locomotive from Cadley Hill Colliery along with a larger preserved steam locomotive if possible.

Coalville Open Day 1986. Photo: John Tuffs.

A big step forward from 1978 were the catering arrangements. There had been some complaints that the catering for the first open day were unsatisfactory, a view recognised by the committee. For 1979, and all the open days thereafter, catering was organised by Walter Tookey and his wife and their helpers. They did a magnificent and very professional job, which was greatly appreciated by the public and all of the open day staff. Again the crowds came out and the attendance was increased on the 1978 show.

After the 1979 open day it was decided that the event would not take place in 1980. Therefore 1981 was selected and the formula was repeated. The Open Days then continued in 1983, 1985 and then annually until the final one was held in 1991.

It had long been thought that one of the problems in boosting the attendance figures was because Coalville was not an easy place to get to, particularly on Sundays. A special bus was laid on between Leicester and Coalville, but was not as well supported as expected.

A train service was the obvious answer, but Coalville had no station or platform. After various meetings the construction of a temporary platform was agreed and authority given for a special passenger service to operate along the branch from Leicester and Burton. This service immediately doubled attendance figures and thereafter they increased every year. Another spin-off from the construction of the platform was that charter train operators, Pathfinder Tours and Hertfordshire Railtours, immediately requested to operate charter trains to the open day. These were very welcome and certainly put Coalville firmly on the map! These enthusiasts specials came every year including 1991 when the last open day was held.

The running of a special passenger service and charter trains over a long low-speed branch line, together with a lengthy single line from Desford to Knighton and short platform constraints at Coalville, meant that any late running or incident would play havoc with any schedules - as it did on some occasions!

For the 1983 open day important changes were made.

First of all we had the passenger services and the charter trains. But we made a giant step forward when we got permission for a steam locomotive to haul the exhibits from the Midland Railway Centre at Butterley under its own power. This locomotive was class 4F 0-6-0 No. 4027 in LMS livery. It brought with it a Deltic diesel locomotive, a class 44 and a class 25 locomotive. This opened the door for future events and a major exhibit of subsequent open days was a large steam loco in steam and running past the assembled crowds.

The presence of these steam giants doubled our attendance and we were soon reaching an attendance figure of between eight to ten thousand on each open day. The last open day in 1991 attracted 15000 people!

Following the appearance of 4027 from Butterley, the following steam locomotives visited the open day. Somerset and Dorset class 7F 2-8-0 No 13809 in black LMS livery; Jubilee class 4-6-0 5593 Kolhapur in red LMS livery; Jubilee class 4-6-0 45596 Bahamas in BR green livery;

Coalville Open Day Committee. (left to right standing) Steve Marks, Pete 'Snowy' Hill, John Kenny, David Kirk (left to right on loco) Colin Hadley, Ian Farnfield, Paul Shilcock. Photo: Unknown.

Unveiling of St. Christopher's Railway Home nameplate on 47348 in 1987 with (left to right) Councillor Peter Kane, Doug Taylor - Chairman of St. Christopher's, Cyril Bleasdale - LM Region General Manager, Sam Reed - Area Manager East Midlands. Photo: John Tuffs.

Class A4 4-6-2 4498 Sir Nigel Gresley in LNER blue livery; Class A3 4-6-2 4472 Flying Scotsman in LNER green livery; Princess Royal Class 4-6-2 46203 Princess Margaret Rose in BR maroon livery; Class 4MT 2-6-4T 80080 in BR black livery. Progress and Swiftsure were provided from Cadley Hill Colliery.

From the beginning of the open days the committee and the Coalville depot staff asked if a locomotive could be named there. It took several years before this came to pass. When it did, class 47/3 47348 was named at Coalville by Mr D. Taylor the chairman of St Christopher's Railway Home at Derby. A plaque was also fitted to this locomotive which stated that the naming ceremony had taken place at Coalville Open Day, in recognition of the funds raised for charity.

A further two class 47 locomotives were named at Coalville in 1989 and 1990 by Mr Charles Belcher the British Rail Post Office Business Manager and were named after depots which were part of the Rail Express Systems infrastructure. These were 47634 Holbeck and 47489 Crewe Diesel Depot.

For several open days the Royal Mail provided a Travelling Post Office Vehicle and staff, which was always a very popular exhibit with the general public queueing to see the interior of these comparatively rare vehicles.

The major customers of the depot at Coalville were of course the National Coal Board, Bardon Hill Quarries and Cliffe Hill Quarries. These all supported the open days with practical help, Bardon Hill even delivered some "filler" to enable us to fill in potholes in the yard.

The support of railway enthusiasts and the charter train operators was greatly appreciated by the Committee and local people. The open day became a big day in Coalville itself. Shops that were normally closed were opened specially. Pubs and the fish and chip restaurant (normally closed on Sundays) advertised a special "Open Day Menu" and the town became really busy. The committee always invited the Chairman of North West District Council to attend and I personally conducted him around the site.

The support and encouragement received from the Council was very welcome. The local press always attended and photographs taken at the open day and a full report was always published. Between 1978 and 1991 eleven open days were held at Coalville, raising £94,000, the majority of which was presented to local and railway charities after our final bills had been cleared. The main railway charities were Derby St Christopher's Railway Home and Condover Hall, but many other charities local to Coalville also benefited. The original idea had far exceeded my wildest dreams.

The Committee had several new members over the years, all of them gave freely of their own time, and as new staff came to the depot they soon became very committed to it. Colin Hadley did a superb job as Treasurer, after succeeding Ian Briggs, and took on many things in addition to his treasurer's duties.

From its inception the open day received encouragement and support from senior railway officials, from the London Midland Region General Manager, down through the Divisional Manager at Nottingham and to the Area Manager at Derby and their successors. In later years this support was supplemented by the Special Trains Manager at British Railways Board HQ, and by the Area Freight Manager at East Midlands Freight. The encouragement and support of all these gentlemen were invaluable and greatly appreciated.

The railway preservation movement itself also gave full support. Approaches to Butterley, the Birmingham Railway Museum and various owners for the loan of their locomotives were always received with enthusiasm. The locomotives were always turned out in an immaculate condition and were a great credit to their owners and support staff.

Enthusiasts were well catered for by the numerous trade stands, all arranged by Mike Evans. Every yard of allocated space was taken and there was always a long waiting list of groups and traders who were keen to attend.

The participation and enthusiasm of the staff gave them all a sense of pride in the depot, and their jobs. Although I have named certain key people, there are many others who did a large amount of work and whose contribution was equally important. This was teamwork of the highest quality. Without the staff, their wives and helpers these open days could never have been the success they were.

David J Kirk BEM, former Traffic Manager Coalville

The Coalville Guards

I had the privilege of representing the guards at Mantle Lane as staff side secretary of the traffic grades LDC from 1980 until closure as a guards depot in July 1988. These were difficult times, as we fought a rearguard action against never-ending cutbacks and the transfer of work away from Coalville. It was probably with these cuts in mind that the majority of guards backed the NUR's call to ban the movement of coal during the NUM dispute of 1984/1985.

(L. to R) R. Baba, D. Wright, G. Cross, J. Wardle, R. Butlin, K. Tilson, R. Clarke and P. Southwood.

First published in the Transport Review. Courtesy of the NUR.

After the end of the strike - or Arthur Scargill's 'Charge of the Light Brigade,' as one guard called it - management took revenge. Driver Only Operation was introduced in several stages until our depot became one of the first to be fully DOO. Happily, no one was made compulsorily redundant; some voluntary redundancies were taken, but many of the guards transferred to depots such as Birmingham New Street and Northampton. Some of them, myself included, became drivers following the October 1988 train crew agreement. Others remained at Coalville and Drakelow Power Station as ground staff and the last duty we performed as an LDC was obtaining a shunter's job for a young lad who'd come in off the street. So many had transferred there were not enough men to fill the vacancies!

Despite the upheavals, Coalville was a happy depot and I'm sure many others look back with great fondness on our time at what was one of the oldest depots in the country. When I started as a guard in 1976 the majority of trains were un-braked apart from the engine and brake van. In fact the only thing that had changed from steam days was the motive power. Most of the unfitted freight trains finished in spring 1981 due to changes in unloading practices at Drakelow A+B and Willington power stations. MGR wagons became the norm and as no brake van was required this practice paved the way for eventual DOO.

In paying tribute to all the guards at Coalville I'd like to name every one of them. Space precludes this, but some spring immediately to mind. Doug Elliot for all his charity work on the Open Day Committee; the incomparable Harry 'Dickey Bow' Johnson who retired as a driver aged 65 and then worked as a guard until his late 70s (I had the honour of firing for Harry on the Great Central Railway in 1977 on the occasion of his 60th year as a railwayman!); my LDC colleagues Peter Hartshorn, Roy Butlin, Graham Cross; and Aubrey Widdowson who as a signalman member of the LDC who agitated constantly for reintroduction of the passenger service long before councillors jumped on the bandwagon and made such a hash of the Ivanhoe Line. Who knows, maybe one-day passenger trains will run again through Coalville and maybe even Coalville depot will re-open.

To close, I would like to thank Tony Gregory for actually preparing this book and I am sure that everyone will enjoy it.

Dennis Wright, Secretary LDC. 'C staff side 1980-88 Coalville

The Leicester Line in the 1980s

The Leicester Line goes from Burton-on-Trent to Knighton Junction and is just less than thirty miles in length. Coalville is situated approximately half way along. The branch comes off the main Derby-Birmingham line at **Leicester Junction**, where a signalbox once stood outside Burton loco sheds (17B/16F). As the route curves eastwards it is joined by a spur line at **Birmingham Curve Junction**. Crossing the old A38 road it then passes over the River Trent via a 16-arch viaduct.

Drakelow Power Station is accessed through Drakelow West arrival, which lies alongside the down departure. During the time of this book it was accessed by the Stanlow oil tanks and Pressflow fly-ash trains. A night tripper sometimes arrived to replace crippled wagons, which were then taken for repair at Burton MGR. The west line then joins the sidings and meets with the east arrival and departure. These lines were even busier, with constant use by coal trains from various locations along the branch.

In the early 1980s class 20s would trip trains of conventional wagons into A/B sidings, from where CEGB shunters would take them for unloading at the mechanical loading plant, which actually lifted and tipped each wagon. After having a brake van attached the 20s would then take away empties for reloading. All these movements were signalled by small semaphores controlled from a shunt frame. A/B was later turned into a Merry-Go-Round circuit. A loaded train entered the circuit and departed after unloading without having to run round. Apart from Drakelow's A/B station the only other MGR circuit I knew of was at Ratcliffe power station. C-station used the same method but required trains to be run round.

The complex was built on the site of Drakelow Hall, once owned by the Gresley family who resided in the area since Norman times. Their most famous son was railway engineer Sir Nigel Gresley. The power station was built in three phases. A-station was started in 1950 and completed in 1955. It closed in 1984. The building of B-station commenced in 1955 and was completed in 1960. The final phase, C-station, was begun in 1960 and finally inaugurated in 1966. For some years the biggest power-generating complex in Europe, Drakelow has dominated the skyline of Burton for over forty years and, at the time of writing, is still going strong.

After leaving Drakelow the next significant spot is **Swadlincote Junction**. From here a line went to Bretby, but this had closed long before my time. Another line went to **Cadley Hill Colliery**, which was turning out vast amounts of coal right up until the early 1980s. Trains were in and out of the place all the time during the week. Access to the branch was by a ground frame worked by a shunter (usually Bud Abbot) who then gave the driver a token to authorise him onto the branch - a practise that ceased in the mid-1980s. Another ground frame was worked to gain access to the full side.

Cadley Hill is noteworthy as one of the last NCB collieries to use steam power. The locos were:

◆ Cadley Hill No.1
◆ No.2 (3059 Florence, as known at former colliery))
◆ 3061 Empress
◆ 7298 Progress
◆ 3851
◆ All yellow spares loco No.65 or 3889.

Runt of the litter was a Sentinel diesel. The engines were kept busy shunting empty and loaded coal trucks and had their own steam shed for maintenance. Enthusiasts and photographers came from far and wide to view and photograph one of the last bastions of colliery steam. The mine finally closed in 1988,

Further along the branch, on the down side Moira end of **Gresley Tunnel**, was the opencast mine of **Swains Park**. It began life in late 1979 and remained in use until the mid-1980s when it was mothballed and eventually demolished. We took empties to the top of the yard and stabled, before taking yet another loaded train out. Swains Park had a man-made incline so loaders were issued with a brake stick and 'gravity-loaded' the trains.

1983. 56067 in Rawdon Colliery prior to departing for Garston Docks. Photo: John Tuffs.

A few hundred yards beyond was **Moira West** signalbox. It controlled trains from the east end of the tunnel and accepted them from Derby power box. Trains were then offered to Mantle Lane signalbox from a colour light starter signal at **Moira**. This once busy but lonely outpost controlled movements in and out of Swains Park, Overseal and Rawdon by use of a mixture of semaphores and colour lights.

Alongside **Overseal Sidings** a number of derelict buildings could be glimpsed amongst the trees. These were all that remained of Overseal sheds, once a sub-depot of Burton. Never home to any more than six or seven engines at most the shed closed in the summer of 1964.

Until the mid 80s the branch went as far as **Measham** and **Donisthorpe**, from where coal was tripped out on a daily basis. Some years earlier it went as far as **Abbey Junction** (Nuneaton). The line was once very busy and passed through, amongst other places, **Shackerstone**, home of the popular private railway **The Battlefield Line**.

Across from the Moira box was **Rawdon Colliery**, where a small single line led to a concrete loading bunker. This once busy place loaded train after train throughout the day. It also had its own loco to bring coal from the pit-head to the storage sidings. In the mid to late 1980s Coalville men worked trains of household coal from Rawdon to Garston Docks in Liverpool, from where it was despatched to Ireland. Coal for the power stations was loaded from the bunker while the wagons were moved forward at half mph by use of slow-speed equipment fitted to the locos.

Lounge open-cast mine opened in the late 1980s. Trains were at first pad-loaded, but a bunker similar to the one at Rawdon was later commissioned. The mine's name was supposedly derived from its location between the two villages of Lount and Tonge.

As the area was remodelled around the new M42 a bridge was slotted in to carry the line. New signalling was also brought in to enable trains to enter from either the Burton or Coalville direction. Prior to that there had been a very long signal section from Moira's colour light to Mantle Lane's home signal. A fixed distant stood near the site of the old station at **Swannington**.

After the crossing at **Hough Hill** we approach Coalville itself. On the left is the old West End shunting neck where, in the 1980s, a coal train ran away down 'The Lickey' (our nickname for No.1 road Mantle Lane). The two Class 20s in charge smashed through the stop-block and buried themselves buffer height in soil!

Mantle Lane signalbox worked all the movements around Coalville. Next to it was **Mantle Lane Sidings**, used primarily for the storage of loads. A pond caused by mining subsidence separated this yard from another yard - the 'long side' -, which was used to back empties into. Across the line was Coalville traincrew depot, which consisted of offices, messroom, washroom and lockers. The engine holding sidings consisted of No.1 and No.2, shedside, shedroad, which ran through the goods shed, and the dock. Attached to the goods shed was the stores. Back on the upside went the shunting neck under the box and almost up to Coalville crossing. A spur went into Marcrofts wagon repair yard, which was situated almost on the site of the old Coalville steam shed (17C) that lay behind the station. According to records, loco-servicing facilities dated back to the 1860s, though the brick-built shed, consisting of three roads and one through road, wasn't completed until the 1890s. The first official ASLEF branch was founded in October 1910, and though it had just five drivers at first it soon grew. The steam shed finally closed on 4th October 1965 and the new traincrew depot was relocated to Mantle Lane.

A stone's throw from the old steam depot, the town's **Coalville Crossing signalbox** controlled the gates that spanned the A50. Formerly known as Coalville Town the whole box stood on a raised platform giving the signalman/crossing-keeper an unbeatable view of his domain. Built in 1907, it superseded an earlier Midland-style box. Coalville Crossing box closed in late 1986 and Mantle Lane took over on 21st December the same year.

47119 Cricklewood - Cliffe Hill passes Bagworth whilst sister loco 47350 awaits departure with a loaded MGR train. Photo: John Tuffs.

In the centre of town was **Snibstone Colliery**. Coal was shipped up the short branch to the ' Top End' sidings by NCB engines, and from there Class 20s tripped the wagons down to Mantle Lane to await their journeys further afield. We also backed empties into **Snibstone Sidings** and the single road on the other side known as Whitwick. Both sidings were accessed by use of a ground frame.

Further east, off **Coalville Junction**, was the single line branch to **Coalfields Farm**, an open-cast site adjacent to the village of Hugglescote. Due to mining subsidence the branch was like an extended Big Dipper, falling steeply and then rising at the same rate. All run-rounds were accessed by a ground frame. This was operated by a shunter up until the mid-1980s, when it became a guards job. Coalfields had its own small shunter but it was rarely seen outside of its shed.

The next port of call was **Bardon Hill Sidings**. Access was by a ground frame which was released by **Bardon Hill signalbox**. The yard was shared by loaded stone wagons from Bardon Quarry and Prismo bitumen tanks from Ellesmere Port that disgorged their sticky loads into waiting lorries. Stone was tripped from the quarry across the A50 road and secured in the yard, then the empties were taken back up - routine tasks that were performed by the quarry's own locos.

Half a mile on the up side was **Cliffe Hill Loading Bunker**. Wagons were filled here by use of a moveable chute. Amongst the trains loaded here in the Eighties were our 6V76 'Hayes & Harlington', two daily Bescot trains, and the 'Doncaster'. Crewed by Derby men, these latter trains were examined at Coalville before commencing their journey. Cliffe Hill closed in

1989 and the huge quarry complex known as Stud Farm opened, taking over the loading of all Cliffe Hill trains.

Bagworth Loading Bunker - completed towards the end of 1979 - was fed by a conveyor belt which crossed the open fields from **Nailstone Colliery**. This operation had a life of just under ten years. Below the bunker site lay Bagworth village. The station there closed in 1964, as did all passenger services on the branch. By the early 1980s only the footbridge, sidings and box remained (though the latter closed with the opening of the new bunker).

Leaving Bagworth the line falls heavily towards the village of **Desford**, home of the huge **Desford Colliery** complex. In the early 1980s Desford coal was taken to Didcot or Rugeley via the south Leicester. Sometimes we were required to bring coal to or via Coalville but with Class 47s being the usual motive power at that time a banker would be required for the challenging Desford bank.

From Desford a very long single-line section winds its way to **Knighton**. Just before Saffron Lane, on the left-hand side, is a single line which once led to the old **Braunston Gate Goods Yard**, later known to rail enthusiasts simply as Vic Berry's. The well-known scrap dealer bought his first consignment of redundant mineral wagons in 1973. So many arrived after that he was forced to stack them five high! This same method was used to store locomotive bodies as they awaited the cutter's torch - the famous 'stack' which could be seen from the Leicester line. Diesel enthusiasts had never seen such a sight and it inevitably invited comparisons with the legendary Dai Woodham's steam graveyard at Barry Island. People came from miles around. Some just for a last glimpse of their favourite engines, others to make a firm cash offer in order to secure the locos for preservation.

At last we arrive at **Knighton Junction** and come to a stand at the junction signal. We sit and wait for the road. (Time for a chat and a cup of tea perhaps?) At last the signal wire tightens, the semaphore goes up, and with a friendly wave from the bobby we're on our way. Alas these things are now just a memory. The box and the semaphores disappeared in 1986. The area is now controlled by colour lights and the sidings just a mess of weeds and rusty rails.

After the closure of Coalville in 1990 the Author transferred to Bescot depot then Saltley in Birmingham staying in the West Midlands for 10 years before transferring to Toton in 2000.

After a couple of years he transferred to Derby 4 Shed on express trains from London to Leeds.

In 2012 he left Derby returning to the freight side of the Railway going back to his roots, and after a few turbulent years and a time with FLHH, was made redundant in 2016 due to closure of the pits and the turn against king coal.

After having a final crack of the whip within the Railway he retired in December 2016 and is at present looking for a small local job.

THE LEICESTER LINE

AS IT WAS IN THE LATE 1970's,
EARLY 1980's Marked *
Others marked with the approximate year

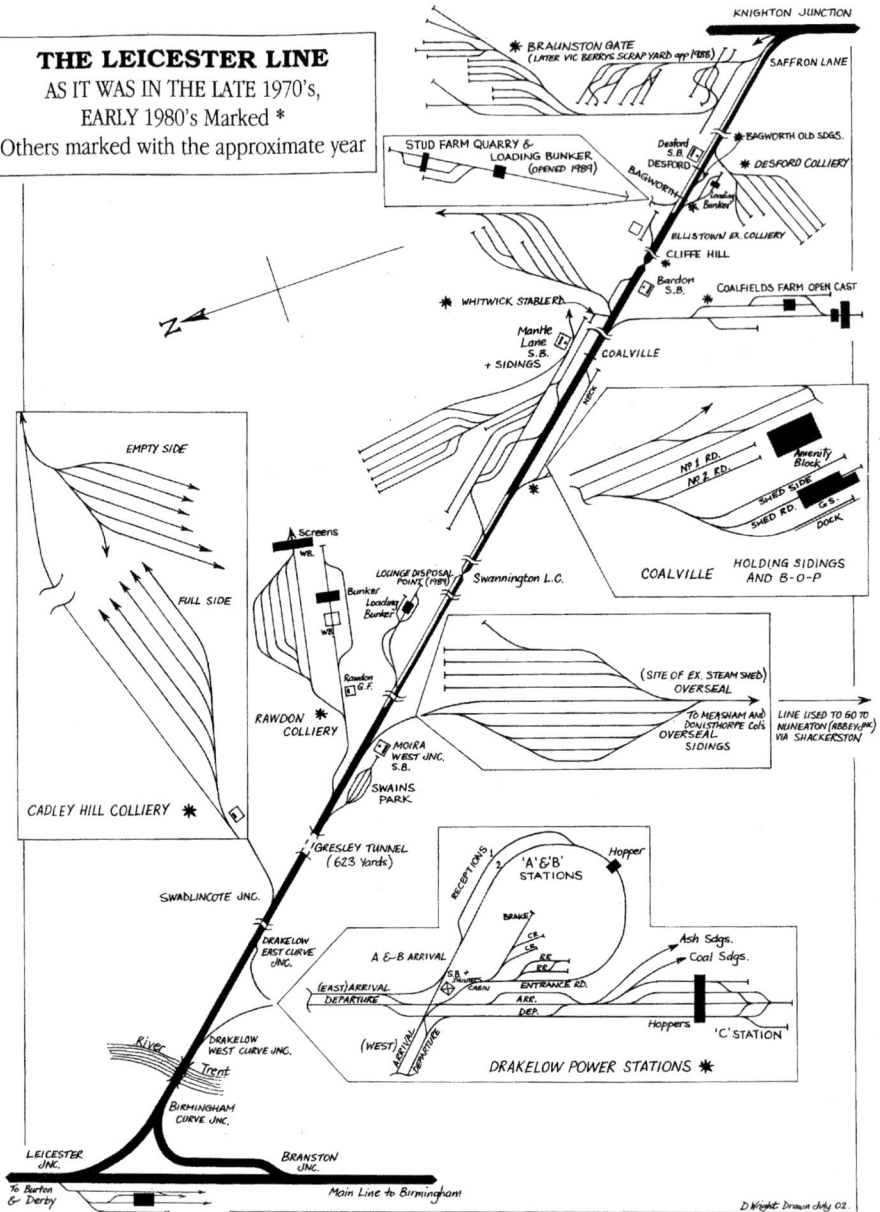

KNIGHTON JUNCTION

* BRAUNSTON GATE
(LATER VIC BERRYS SCRAP YARD app 1988)

SAFFRON LANE

STUD FARM QUARRY &
LOADING BUNKER (OPENED 1989)

* BAGWORTH OLD SDGS.

Desford
S.B.
DESFORD

* DESFORD COLLIERY

BAGWORTH

Loading
Bunker

ELLISTOWN EX. COLLIERY

CLIFFE HILL

Bardon
S.B.

COALFIELDS FARM OPEN CAST

* WHITWICK STABLE RD.

Mantle
Lane
S.B.
+ SIDINGS

COALVILLE

NECK

No 1 RD.
No 2 RD.

Amenity
Block

SHED SIDE
SHED RD.
G.S.

DOCK

EMPTY SIDE

COALVILLE

HOLDING SIDINGS
AND B-O-P

FULL SIDE

Screens
W.R.

LOUNGE DISPOSAL
POINT (1989)

Swannington L.C.

Bunker
Loading
Bunker

W.R.

(SITE OF EX. STEAM SHED)
OVERSEAL

Rawdon
G.F.

TO MEASHAM AND
DONISTHORPE Cols.

LINE USED TO GO TO
NUNEATON (ABBEY JNC)
VIA SHACKERSTON

RAWDON
COLLIERY

OVERSEAL
SIDINGS

MOIRA
WEST JNC.
S.B.

SWAINS
PARK

CADLEY HILL COLLIERY *

GRESLEY TUNNEL
(623 yards)

RECEPTIONS

Hopper

'A' & 'B'
STATIONS

SWADLINCOTE JNC.

BRAKE

CE
LB
RE
RR

Ash Sdgs.

Coal Sdgs.

DRAKELOW
EAST CURVE
JNC.

A & B ARRIVAL

S.B. +
SHUNTERS
CABIN

ENTRANCE RD.

ARR.
DEP.

(EAST) ARRIVAL
DEPARTURE

Hoppers

'C' STATION

DRAKELOW
WEST CURVE JNC.

(WEST)

ARRIVAL
DEPARTURE

DRAKELOW POWER STATIONS *

River
Trent

BIRMINGHAM
CURVE JNC.

LEICESTER
JNC.

BRANSTON
JNC.

To Burton
& Derby

Main Line to Birmingham

D Wright Drawn July 02.